The Prophecies of Daniel
According to Kabbalah

CHAPTER 8
Alternate Translation©

For My Parents
Louis and Evelyn Goldstein

Copyright © 2015 by Christ-Centered Kabbalah
All rights reserved under International Copyright Law.
Published @ Long Island, NY March, 2015

ISBN: 13: 978-0692415603
ISBN: 10: 0692415602

**The Prophecies of Daniel According to Kabbalah
Chapter 8, Alternate Translation**
Sheila R. Vitale

No part of this book may be reproduced, in any form,
without written permission from the publisher

Requests for permission to reproduce selections
from this book should be mailed to:

Christ-Centered Kabbalah

Sheila R. Vitale
P O Box 562
Port Jefferson Station, NY 11776-0562 USA
(631) 331-1493

TABLE OF AUTHORITIES

1. **Brown Driver & Briggs' Hebrew Lexicon**, Woodside Bible Fellowship, Ontario, Canada, Licensed From The Institute for Creation Research.

2. **Englishman's Greek-Hebrew Concordance.**

3. **Gesenius' Hebrew and Chaldee Lexicon to the Old Testament** Scriptures, Baker Book House, Grand Rapids, Michigan.

4. **The Interlinear Bible** (Jay P. Green, Sr.), Hendrickson Publisher's, Peabody, Massachusetts 01961-3473.

5. **The Interlinear Bible (transliterated), Biblesoft and International Bible Translators, Inc.**

6. **Nave's Topical Bible.**

7. **Nelson's Bible Dictionary**, Thomas Nelson, Inc., Publishers, Nashville, Tennessee.

8. **Strong's Exhaustive Concordance** (James Strong) Thomas Nelson, Inc., Publishers, Nashville, Tennessee.

9. **Strong's Hebrew And Chaldee Dictionary** (James Strong), Thomas Nelson, Inc., Publishers, Nashville, Tennessee.

10. **Strong's Greek Dictionary** (James Strong), Thomas Nelson, Inc., Publishers, Nashville, Tennessee.

11. **The New Thayer's Greek-English Lexicon Of The New Testament**, Hendrickson Publisher's, Peabody, Massachusetts 01961-3473.

12. **Unger's Bible Dictionary** (Merrill F. Unger), The Moody Bible Institute of Chicago, Chicago, Illinois 60610.

13. **1979 Authorized Version** (AV), The On-Line Bible

14. **Stephanus Greek Text,** The On-Line Bible

15. **Green's Literal Translation,** The On-Line Bible

Christ-Centered Kabbalah
Sheila R. Vitale
Pastor, Teacher, Founder
PO Box 562
Port Jefferson Station, NY 11776 USA

The Prophecies of Daniel
According to Kabbalah

CHAPTER 8
Alternate Translation©

The Alternate Translation of
Daniel, Chapter 8
was rendered in Parts 1-5 of
CCK Message #831, A History of Adam

**Edited and Adapted as a Book by
Sheila R. Vitale**

Formatted as a Book by
The CCK Administrative Professional Staff

Christ-Centered Kabbalah
~ The Compleat Kabbalah ~
Sheila R. Vitale
Pastor, Teacher & Founder

Ministry Staff
Anthony Milton, Teacher (South Carolina)
Brooke Paige, Teacher (New York)
Sandra Aldrich (MN) (July 7, 1975 – April 18, 2021)

Administrative Staff
Susan Panebianco, Office Manager

Editorial Staff
Rose Herczeg, Editor

Technical Staff
Lape Mobolaji-Lawal, Database Administrator

Ministry Illustrators
Cecilia H. Bryant (Oct. 18, 1921 – Oct. 23, 2013)
Fidelis Onwubueke

Music Staff
June Eble, Singer, Lyricist and Clarinetist
(July 20, 1931 – Jan. 24, 2024)
Don Gervais, Singer, Lyricist and Guitarist
Rita L. Rora, Singer, Lyricist and Guitarist

Table of Contents

ALTERNATE TRANSLATIONS IN THIS BOOK .... B

PREFACE I

    WHY ANOTHER TRANSLATION? I
    PREPARING TO TRANSLATE III
    ALTERNATE TRANSLATIONS ARE PROGRESSIVE IV
    THE TORAH (THE WORD OF GOD) IS ALIVE IV

KING JAMES TRANSLATION 1

DANIEL 8:1-27 ALTERNATE AMPLIFIED TRANSLATION 5

    THE VISION 5
    TWO SOURCES OF POWER 5
    ADAM, UNSTOPPABLE 6
    TWO MALES 6
    A LARGE LIZARD 6
    ADAM'S POWER BROKEN 7
    MARRYING THE FEMALES 7
    A BONE CRUNCHING VICTORY 7
    A SEED GOES FORTH 7
    THE ARMIES OF HEAVEN 8
    MICHAEL, THE PRINCE 8
    THE ATONEMENT 8
    HOW LONG 8
    ADAM CALLS GABRIEL 9
    A VISION ABOUT THE END TIMES 9
    CAIN'S RAGE 9
    ELOHIM DIVIDED 9
    THE MUD KING 10
    ADAM FALLEN 10
    THE SHEKINAH IS SUFFICIENT 10
    PROCREATIVE SPIRITUAL POWER 10
    THE LIZARD DEFEATED 11
    THE PRINCE OF PRINCES 11
    A VISION FOR THE FUTURE 11
    DANIEL'S SICKNESS 11

FOOTNOTED VERSION DANIEL 8:1-27 ALTERNATE AMPLIFIED TRANSLATION 13

- The Vision 13
- Two Sources of Power 14
- Adam, Unstoppable 15
- Two Males 16
- A Large Lizard 16
- Adam's Power Broken 17
- Marrying the Females 18
- A Bone Crunching Victory 18
- A Seed Goes Forth 19
- The Armies of Heaven 19
- Michael, the Prince 20
- The Atonement 20
- How Long 20
- Adam Calls Gabriel 21
- A Vision About the End Times 22
- Cain's Rage 22
- Elohim Divided 22
- The Mud King 23
- Adam Fallen 23
- The Shekinah Is Sufficient 23
- Procreative Spiritual Power 24
- The Lizard Defeated 24
- The Prince of Princes 25
- A Vision For the Future 25
- Daniel's Sickness 25

APPENDICES 27

- Appendix - Verse 1 31
  - No Lecture Notes 31
  - Reference Scriptures for Verse 1 31
- Appendix - Verse 2 32
  - Footnotes 32
  - Lecture Notes for Verse 2 33
  - Reference Scriptures for Verse 2 34
- Appendix - Verse 3 36
  - Footnotes 36
  - Lecture Notes for Verse 3 36
  - Reference Scriptures for Verse 3 38
- Appendix - Verse 4 39
  - Footnotes 39
  - Lecture Notes for Verse 4 39
  - Reference Scriptures for Verse 4 41

APPENDIX - VERSE 5	42
Footnotes	42
Lecture Notes for Verse 5	45
APPENDIX - VERSE 6	47
Footnotes	47
Lecture Notes For Verse 6	47
Reference Scriptures for Verse 6	48
APPENDIX - VERSE 7	49
Lecture Notes For Verse #7	49
Reference Scriptures for Verse 7	50
APPENDIX - VERSE 8	51
Footnotes	51
Lecture Notes For Verse 8	52
Reference Scriptures for Verse 8	53
APPENDIX - VERSE 9	54
Footnotes	54
Lecture Notes For Verse 9	54
Reference Scriptures for Verse 9	55
APPENDIX - VERSE 10	56
Footnotes	56
Lecture Notes For Verse 10	57
Reference Scriptures for Verse 10	57
APPENDIX - VERSE 11	59
Lecture Notes for Verse 11	59
Reference Scriptures for Verse 11	60
APPENDIX - VERSE 12	61
Lecture Notes For Verse 12	61
Reference Scriptures for Verse 12	62
APPENDIX – VERSE 13	65
Lecture Notes For Verse 13	65
Reference Scriptures for Verse 13	66
APPENDIX – VERSE 14	67
Footnotes	67
Lecture Notes For Verse 14	68
Reference Scriptures for Verse 14	69
APPENDIX – VERSE 15	70
Lecture Notes For Verse 15	70
APPENDIX – VERSE 16	71
Footnotes	71
Reference Scriptures for Verse 16	73
APPENDIX – VERSE 17	74
Lecture Notes For Verse 17	74
APPENDIX – VERSE 18	75
Lecture Notes For Verse 18	75

APPENDIX – VERSE 19 76
   Footnotes 76
   Lecture Notes For Verse 19 76
   Reference Scriptures for Verse 19 77
APPENDIX – VERSE 20 78
   Footnotes 78
   Lecture Notes For Verse 20 78
APPENDIX – VERSE 21 84
   Footnotes 84
   Lecture Notes For Verse 21 84
APPENDIX – VERSE 22 86
   Footnotes 86
   Lecture Notes For Verse 22 86
   Reference Scriptures for Verse 22 87
APPENDIX – VERSE 23 88
   Footnotes 88
   Lecture Notes For Verse 23 88
APPENDIX – VERSE 24 91
   Lecture Notes For Verse 24 91
APPENDIX – VERSE 25 92
   Footnotes 92
   Lecture Notes For Verse 25 92
   Reference Scriptures for Verse 25 93
APPENDIX – VERSE 26 94
   Lecture Notes For Verse 26 94
APPENDIX – VERSE 27 95
   Footnotes 95
   Lecture Notes For Verse 27 95

TABLE OF REFERENCES 97

ABOUT THE AUTHOR 99

The Alternate Translation Bible©

The Alternate Translation Bible **(ATB)** is an original translation of the Scripture.

Alternate Translation of the Old Testament©
Alternate Translation, Exodus, Chapter 32
(Crime of the Calf)©
Alternate Translation, Daniel, Chapter 8©
Alternate Translation, Daniel, Chapter 11©

Alternate Translation of the New Testament©
Alternate Translation, 2 Thessalonians, Chapter 2
    (Sophia)©
Alternate Translation, 1st John, Chapter 5©
Alternate Translation, the Book of Colossians
    (To The Church At Colosse)
Alternate Translation, the Book of Corinthians, Chapter 11
    (Corinthian Confusion)
Alternate Translation, the Book of Jude
    (The Common Salvation)©

Alternate Translation of the Book of the Revelation of Jesus Christ
    to St. John©
Traducción Alternada del Libro de Revelación de Jesucristo©

Alternate Translations In This Book

DANIEL 8:1-27	5
GENESIS 2:18	45
GENESIS 1:7-8	69
2 COR 4:6-7	72
GENESIS 2:18	72

The Prophecies of Daniel
According to Kabbalah

CHAPTER 8
Alternate Translation©

PREFACE

Why Another Translation?

The King James Translators were not spiritual men. They were scholars who, themselves, perceived the Deity of the Scripture as an unforgiving, punishing God. But there is another Message, a spiritual understanding of the Scripture called *the Doctrine of Christ*, which reveals a loving God, whose sole intention towards mankind is to deliver us from destruction and death.

There are many definitions for each word in the English dictionary, and many translations for each Hebrew and Greek word in the original text of the Scripture.

The King James Translators dealt with the problem of one Hebrew source word appearing several times in a single Chapter, by using a different English word each time that the Hebrew word appears. The English word choices of the translator, then, are directly related to 1) his knowledge of the Word of God, 2) the degree to which he is influenced by the Spirit of Revelation and 3) the accepted understanding of the Word of God at the time.

The Spirit of Revelation influences the translator to choose legitimate *Alternate Translations* from the Hebrew and Greek lexicons listed in the front of *The Prophecies of Daniel According to Kabbalah, Chapter 8, Alternate Translation*, to express the spiritual intent of the Scripture. The Alternate English Translations for some of the Hebrew words in the Scripture are just as legitimate as the choices made by the King James Translators, but they render a radically different, and much more positive Translation than the Authorized Version.

Multiple English translations for the same Hebrew word in the King James text are perfectly legitimate examples of Translator's License, and simply prove our point: *The King James Translators, themselves, used multiple definitions of the same Hebrew Word.*

The Prophecies of Daniel According to Kabbalah, Chapter 8, is a Spiritual Translation of the Scripture, which is as legitimate to the Spiritual Mind, as the King James translation is to the Carnal Mind. The *Alternate Translation Bi*ble sounds radically different than the King James and other translations, because it must be Spiritually Discerned (1 Cor. 2:14).

A knowledge of the True Intent of the author of the Scripture, and a desire to understand the message that he intended to convey, should be the top priority for all genuine seekers of *Truth.*

God is the Living Word that feeds Mankind through imperfect vessels. Beware of idolatry for the King James, or any other Translation, because *all translations* are the work of imperfect, mortal men. Seek God and He will direct your paths (Pro. 3:6).

May the Spirit of Truth expose all of our wrong thinking, and may the Truth intended by the author of the Word cleave to our heart and mind, because the Spirit of Truth awakens our potential for Eternal Life (1 Cor 15:4).

Romans 8:1-14

1. THERE IS THEREFORE NOW NO CONDEMNATION TO THEM WHICH ARE IN CHRIST JESUS, WHO WALK NOT AFTER THE FLESH, BUT AFTER THE SPIRIT.

2. FOR THE LAW OF THE SPIRIT OF LIFE IN CHRIST JESUS HATH MADE ME FREE FROM THE LAW OF SIN AND DEATH.

3. FOR WHAT THE LAW COULD NOT DO, IN THAT IT WAS WEAK THROUGH THE FLESH, GOD SENDING HIS OWN SON IN THE LIKENESS OF SINFUL FLESH, AND FOR SIN, CONDEMNED SIN IN THE FLESH:

4. THAT THE RIGHTEOUSNESS OF THE LAW MIGHT BE FULFILLED IN US, WHO WALK NOT AFTER THE FLESH, BUT AFTER THE SPIRIT.

5. FOR THEY THAT ARE AFTER THE FLESH DO MIND THE THINGS OF THE FLESH; BUT THEY THAT ARE AFTER THE SPIRIT THE THINGS OF THE SPIRIT.

6. FOR TO BE CARNALLY MINDED IS DEATH; BUT TO BE SPIRITUALLY MINDED IS LIFE AND PEACE.

7. BECAUSE THE CARNAL MIND IS ENMITY AGAINST GOD: FOR IT IS NOT SUBJECT TO THE LAW OF GOD, NEITHER INDEED CAN BE.

8. SO THEN THEY THAT ARE IN THE FLESH CANNOT PLEASE GOD.

9. BUT YE ARE NOT IN THE FLESH, BUT IN THE SPIRIT, IF SO BE THAT THE SPIRIT OF GOD DWELL IN YOU. NOW IF ANY MAN HAVE NOT THE SPIRIT OF CHRIST, HE IS NONE OF HIS.

10. AND IF CHRIST BE IN YOU, THE BODY IS DEAD BECAUSE OF SIN; BUT THE SPIRIT IS LIFE BECAUSE OF RIGHTEOUSNESS.

11. BUT IF THE SPIRIT OF HIM THAT RAISED UP JESUS FROM THE DEAD DWELL IN YOU, HE THAT RAISED UP CHRIST FROM THE DEAD SHALL ALSO QUICKEN YOUR MORTAL BODIES BY HIS SPIRIT THAT DWELLETH IN YOU.

12. THEREFORE, BRETHREN, WE ARE DEBTORS, NOT TO THE FLESH, TO LIVE AFTER THE FLESH.

FOR IF YE LIVE AFTER THE FLESH, YE SHALL DIE: BUT IF YE THROUGH THE SPIRIT DO MORTIFY THE DEEDS OF THE BODY, YE SHALL LIVE.

Preparing To Translate

The Prophesies of Daniel According to Kabbalah, Chapter 8, Alternate Translation, was researched in March of 2015, and preached in two separate meetings as *Christ-Centered Kabbalah* Message #831, *A History of Adam.*

Three Hebrew-English dictionaries, three Interlinear Texts, and multiple Bible Dictionaries (see, Table of Authorities at the beginning of *this Book*) were used to search out the meaning of each Hebrew word of Daniel, Chapter 8. English dictionaries, encyclopedias and search engines, were also employed to acquire as much information as possible about obviously, and not so obviously related topics, which were revealed through the *Alternate Translations.*

Each word and verse was seriously prayed over to discover God's spiritual message behind the written words.

The Prophecies of Daniel, Chapter 8, Accorcing to Kabbalah, Alternate Translation, contains a Table of References, as well as an Appendix for each verse, which includes the Notes created for that verse as CCK Message #831, *A History of Adam,* was preached.

It is not unusual for the verse structure of the *Alternate Translations* to be rearranged so that they can be read as one continuous message. Accordingly, some paragraph numbers are out of order (*3* before *2,* for example) and some paragraphs are divided into *a* and *b* and interspersed (*2a, 3a, 2b, 3b,* for example).

Alternate Translations Are Progressive

Alternate Translations were rendered for each verse in its entirety. After that, all of the translated verses are read together as one whole revelation, to confirm their synchronicity, reveal additional, deep nuances of the whole revelation, and to expose any inconsistencies or errors.

Alternate Translations are progressive in that the *Alternate Translation* for each verse is affected by the *Alternate Translations* for previous and subsequent verses. A newly translated verse, for example, will be influenced by previous Alternate Translations, and sometimes the Alternate Translation for the new verse causes changes in previously translated verses.

The Torah (The Word of God) Is Alive

The *Alternate Translation* of one whole chapter of Scripture is a living organism that evolves and grows in scope. The Spirit of Revelation refines the *Alternate Translations* as the translator reads and re-reads them. Eventually, all of the thoughts, understanding and influences of the Carnal Mind are removed, and the optimal understanding for that particular time, is reached.

Accordingly, you will find several versions of *Daniel, Chapter 8*, in this Book, which represent the progression of the *Alternate Translation* from its beginning to its final stage:

1. The King James Version [KJV]
2. The Alternate, Amplified Translation [ATB]
3. The Alternate Amplified Translation – Annotated [ATB]

Written words are vessels that clothe the spiritual word, just like the body is a vessel that carries the soul in this world. It might even be said that the spiritual understanding of a written word is the soul of that written word.

Unveiling the spiritual meaning of a word shatters its hard exterior, so that the spiritual contents flow out and blend with the spiritual contents of the other vessels. *The Spirit of Revelation* takes hold of the Torah (Word of God) in this *liquid form,* goes beyond the letter of the Word, and reveals the esoteric message of the Torah (Word of God) for a particular people, at an appointed time.

Sheila R. Vitale

DANIEL 8:1-27

KING JAMES TRANSLATION

¹ In the third year of the reign of king Belshazzar a vision appeared unto me, even unto me Daniel, after that which appeared unto me at the first.

² And I saw in a vision; and it came to pass, when I saw, that I was at Shushan in the palace, which is in the province of Elam; and I saw in a vision, and I was by the river of Ulai.

³ Then I lifted up mine eyes, and saw, and, behold, there stood before the river a ram which had two horns: and the two horns were high; but one was higher than the other, and the higher came up last.

⁴ I saw the ram pushing westward, and northward, and southward; so that no beasts might stand before him, neither was there any that could deliver out of his hand; but he did according to his will, and became great.

⁵ And as I was considering, behold, an he goat came from the west on the face of the whole earth, and touched not the ground: and the goat had a notable horn between his eyes.

⁶ And he came to the ram that had two horns, which I had there seen standing before the river, and ran unto him in the fury of his power.

⁷ And I saw him come close unto the ram, and he was moved with choler against him, and smote the ram, and brake his two horns: and there was no power in the ram to stand before him, but he cast him down to the ground, and stamped

The Prophecies Of Daniel According to Kabbalah, Chapter 8/ Daniel 8:1-27
— King James Translation

upon him: and there was none that could deliver the ram out of his hand.

8 Therefore the he goat waxed very great: and when he was strong, the great horn was broken; and for it came up four notable ones toward the four winds of heaven.

9 And out of one of them came forth a little horn, which waxed exceeding great, toward the south, and toward the east, and toward the pleasant land.

10 And it waxed great, even to the host of heaven; and it cast down some of the host and of the stars to the ground, and stamped upon them.

11 Yea, he magnified himself even to the prince of the host, and by him the daily sacrifice was taken away, and the place of his sanctuary was cast down.

12 And an host was given him against the daily sacrifice by reason of transgression, and it cast down the truth to the ground; and it practised, and prospered.

13 Then I heard one saint speaking, and another saint said unto that certain saint which spake, How long shall be the vision concerning the daily sacrifice, and the transgression of desolation, to give both the sanctuary and the host to be trodden under foot?

14 And he said unto me, Unto two thousand and three hundred days; then shall the sanctuary be cleansed.

15 And it came to pass, when I, even I Daniel, had seen the vision, and sought for the meaning, then, behold, there stood before me as the appearance of a man.

16 And I heard a man's voice between the banks of Ulai, which called, and said, Gabriel, make this man to understand the vision.

The Prophecies Of Daniel According to Kabbalah, Chapter 8/ Daniel 8:1-27
– King James Translation

¹⁷ So he came near where I stood: and when he came, I was afraid, and fell upon my face: but he said unto me, Understand, O son of man: for at the time of the end shall be the vision.

¹⁸ Now as he was speaking with me, I was in a deep sleep on my face toward the ground: but he touched me, and set me upright.

¹⁹ And he said, Behold, I will make thee know what shall be in the last end of the indignation: for at the time appointed the end shall be.

²⁰ The ram which thou sawest having two horns are the kings of Media and Persia.

²¹ And the rough goat is the king of Grecia: and the great horn that is between his eyes is the first king.

²² Now that being broken, whereas four stood up for it, four kingdoms shall stand up out of the nation, but not in his power.

²³ And in the latter time of their kingdom, when the transgressors are come to the full, a king of fierce countenance, and understanding dark sentences, shall stand up.

²⁴ And his power shall be mighty, but not by his own power: and he shall destroy wonderfully, and shall prosper, and practise, and shall destroy the mighty and the holy people.

²⁵ And through his policy also he shall cause craft to prosper in his hand; and he shall magnify himself in his heart, and by peace shall destroy many: he shall also stand up against the Prince of princes; but he shall be broken without hand.

²⁶ And the vision of the evening and the morning which was told is true: wherefore shut thou up the vision; for it shall be for many days.

The Prophecies Of Daniel According to Kabbalah, Chapter 8/ Daniel 8:1-27
– King James Translation

27 And I Daniel fainted, and was sick certain days; afterward I rose up, and did the king's business; and I was astonished at the vision, but none understood it.

KJV

DANIEL 8:1-27

ALTERNATE AMPLIFIED TRANSLATION

Introduction

1   In the third year of the reign of King Belshazzar, a vision appeared to me, Daniel, after the first [vision] that appeared to me, and

The Vision

2   I saw a vision [of a] building, [and] the building [that] I saw was the hidden palace of Righteous Adam, the house[hold] of I [AM, and] I saw in the vision that the legal authority of I [AM] was above [the will] of the foolish [sheep], and

Two Sources of Power

3   I lifted up my eyes and there he was! I saw [Righteous Adam], a mighty man [whose] personality [was] the doorway [to the spiritual world of God, and] he was standing by the river [that flows out of Eden, and] he had two sources of power, and [the Shekinah], the first [source of Adam's power], was higher than [the power of her Son, who is] the second [source of Adam's power], and the Shekinah], the higher [source of Adam's power], arose [into this World of Action] last, and

The Prophecies Of Daniel According to Kabbalah, Chapter 8/ Daniel 8:1-27
– Alternate Amplified Translation

Adam, Unstoppable

4   I saw [Righteous Adam], the mighty man [who was the personality of Primordial Adam], the nonexistent one, pushing forth into

         (1)   The [emotional] sea [of the World of Forms (Yetzirah), and into]

         (2)   The hidden, dark place [of the unconscious mind of the female goats], and into

         (3)   The desert [World of Creation (Beriah), where Adam is formed, and]

      He was twisting together with the [female goats, and] the whole living creature could not stand before [Righteous Adam], or deliver [themselves] out of his hand, and [Righteous Adam] did whatever he wanted to do [with the females goats], and

Two Males

5   As I [AM gave me the] understanding [of the vision], there it was! A male Goat and a company of female goats who were collectively male, and [Righteous Adam], the personality of the nonexistent one who comes from the region of the evening sun, [who is] above the whole earth[en creature], had spiritual sexual intercourse with [the female goats who were formed from] the ground, and the male Goat [who had] the power of vision [from the brow energy center] between his eyes, [saw what was happening, and]

A Large Lizard

6   [I saw] a large Lizard rush towards [Righteous Adam], the personality [that] was standing by the river [that flows out of Eden, and] he was enraged, and he came as a husband at [the female side of Righteous Adam], the mighty man who had two sources of power, and

Adam's Power Broken

7   I saw [the Lizard come] near to [the female side of Righteous Adam], the mighty man, [and] have spiritual sexual intercourse with [his female] side, [and when the Lizard] struck [Righteous Adam], the mighty man, [by having spiritual sexual intercourse with his female side, Righteous Adam's] two power sources burst [apart], and there was no strength in [Righteous Adam], the mighty man, to throw the personality of [the male Goat] down to the ground and tread upon him, and there was no [spiritual source powerful enough] to snatch [Righteous Adam], the mighty man, [and his male] drop, away from the spiritual hand [of the Lizard], and

Marrying the Females

8a   The male Goat vehemently twisted [together] with [the gazelle that had Jehovah's nature], in the same manner [that Righteous Adam twisted together with the female goats that had the Lizard's nature],

A Bone Crunching Victory

8b   Daniel saw [in] I [AM's] vision, [that] the widow[ed Adam] became strong enough [to overcome] the great power [of the Lizard, and he saw] the four [faces of Righteous Adam], the Son [of God], ascend [from underneath the personality of the female goat] and replace the four [faces of fallen Adam], and [Daniel] saw [Righteous Adam] crunch the spiritual bones [of the female goat] personality [of the Lizard] that had overthrown his male personality, and

A Seed Goes Forth

9   [Adam's male drop], the little united power, went forth from the part of [Righteous Adam that was] united with [the Shekinah, and it] twisted [together with the human spirit], the

The Prophecies Of Daniel According to Kabbalah, Chapter 8/ Daniel 8:1-27 – Alternate Amplified Translation

superior [part of Abel], the gazelle [that Jehovah formed] in the desert [World of Creation (Beriah), and] [Primordial Adam] the rising sun [of the Third Day of Creation carried it] toward

The Armies of Heaven

10   [The holy ones, and] it twisted together with the armies of heaven, and they cast down some of the princes of the armies of [the Lizard] to the ground, and tread upon them, and

Michael, the Prince

11   The Prince of the armies [of heaven] twisted [together with] the holy ones to raise up the continual sacrifice, and [the armies of heaven] cast down the part of [the Lizard that was occupying] their dwelling places, and

The Atonement

12   The armies [of heaven] pushed forward from above to put the continual sacrifice in place for the rebels [who become goats after] they cast the truth down to the ground, and

How Long

13   Then I heard [Righteous Adam], one holy one, speaking, and [Righteous Adam], the one who spoke, said to [Gabriel], another holy one, [tell Daniel about] the vision, [tell him,] how long [it will take for]

    (1)   The daily [sacrifice and]

    (2)   The rebellion [that] stunned and devastated [Righteous Adam to end, and]

    (3)   To give the holy ones, [Jehovah's] armies, [the power] to tread [the Lizard] under foot, and

The Prophecies Of Daniel According to Kabbalah, Chapter 8/ Daniel 8:1-27
– Alternate Amplified Translation

14   [Gabriel] said to me, [it will take] until the evening and the morning of the Second Day of Creation, [when the Shekinah descends into] the holy ones [to become the Keter, Chochmah and Binah, the upper] triad [of the Son of Adam, the one who] makes [them] righteous, and

15   It came to pass that when Daniel saw I [AM's] vision and sought after the meaning, there it was! A man [who] appeared [to be] a mighty warrior stood opposite him, and

Adam Calls Gabriel

16   [Daniel] heard Adam's voice [coming from] the midst of the solitary, unmarried image [of the warrior], calling him by name, saying, Gabriel, make this foolish [sheep who is my] other self, understand the vision, and

18   I was stunned, [and] as he spoke with me I fell into a trance, and [Gabriel] had spiritual sexual intercourse with my earth[en] personality, [and] stood me upright, and

A Vision About the End Times

17   [Gabriel] said to me, understand, son of Adam, [that] the vision [is about] the end times, and

Cain's Rage

19   [Gabriel] said, look! I will tell you [what] shall come to pass at the appointed time of the end, [when] Elohim, your other self, [shall put] an end [to Cain's] rage, [and what will come to pass concerning]

Elohim Divided

22   (1)   The large Lizard [that] burst [apart the Mother and the Son], the two powers [which were revealed through

The Prophecies Of Daniel According to Kabbalah, Chapter 8/ Daniel 8:1-27
– Alternate Amplified Translation

Righteous Adam] in the [lower] window of [creation where Leviathan], the fish [is], and

(2) The Serpent [who] stood up four nations [in the World of Action (Asiyah)] below [to replace] the four [spiritual] kingdoms [that exist, but] are not standing up [in the visible world yet, and]

The Mud King

21 (3) The king [who] looks like a man, but is formed from the mud [and is really] an hybrid deity [of the household of the Lizard] that has horns, a tail and the hind legs of a goat, and the great power between his two eyes is [Nimrod], the first king, and

Adam Fallen

24a The large Lizard [that empowers the male Goat] shall be mighty, and [Righteous Adam] shall not have the power to separate [himself from the male Goat, but

The Shekinah Is Sufficient

20 The Mother and the Son of the God World of Emanation (Atzilut)], the two sources of power of [Righteous Adam], the mighty man that you saw, are sufficient [to overthrow] the kings who broke into pieces [when they fell down into this world], and

Procreative Spiritual Power

23 In the end time, a king with [spiritual] procreative power and the [spiritual] intelligence to understand the mysteries of the kingdom [of God], shall stand up and complete the personalities of the rebels, and

The Lizard Defeated

24b   The Shekinah] shall push forward [into the earth], and destroy [the Lizard, and Righteous Adam] shall make [the male Goat] a ruin[ous heap, and acquire] a large number of [the female goats, and

The Prince of Princes

25   The Shekinah, Jehovah's] intelligence from above, shall push forward into the heart [center where Righteous Adam is, and they shall form] the mind of peace from above, [which] shall twist together with the ruined [mind of] the counterfeit [Adam], and the Prince of princes shall stand up in the many [members of humanity, and] end the [reptilian] rebellion, and

A Vision For the Future

26   The vision of the evening and the morning [of the Second Day of Creation] which was told to you is true, [but] the vision will not come to pass for many days, so [the understanding of it] will be locked up [until the time appointed for it to come to pass]; and

Daniel's Sickness

27   Daniel was physically weak [for many] days [after Righteous Adam, Gabriel's] mate from above, stood up [in him, because] the wisdom of I [AM] is the creative process that destroys the king[dom of darkness, and Daniel] did not understand the vision.

The Prophecies Of Daniel According to Kabbalah, Chapter 8/ Footnoted Version

FOOTNOTED VERSION

DANIEL 8:1-27

ALTERNATE AMPLIFIED TRANSLATION

Introduction

1   In the third year of the reign of King Belshazzar, a vision appeared to me, Daniel, after the first [vision]^R that appeared to me, and

^{R} Dan 7:2

The Vision

2   I saw a vision [of a] building,$^{R-1}$ [and] the building ^{1} [that] I saw was the hidden palace of Righteous Adam,^{2} the house[hold] of I [AM, and] I saw in the vision that the legal authority of I [AM] was above [the will] of the foolish [sheep],$^{R-2}$ ^{3} and

$^{R-1}$ 1 Ki 8:20
$^{R-2}$ Zech 11:15

---

^{1} The foundation of the spiritual building that God inhabits is in the earth, and the building extends upward into heaven. (1 Cor 3:11)

^{2} Righteous Adam is the house, or the palace, that God lives in, and Righteous Adam lives in humanity, so Righteous Adam is the spiritual man . . . . (Footnote continued in Appendix #2, p *32*).

^{3} The word *foolish* signifies the animal mind, which is the mind of humanity, as opposed to the mind of God. The authority of I AM, the Name of God . . . . (Footnote continued in Appendix #2, p *32*).

The Prophecies Of Daniel According to Kabbalah, Chapter 8/ Footnoted Version

Two Sources of Power

3   I lifted up my eyes and there he was! I saw [Righteous Adam], a mighty man[4] [whose] personality [was] the doorway[R-1] [to the spiritual World of God, and] he was standing by the river [that flows out of Eden,[R-2] and] he had two sources of power,[5] and [the Shekinah],[6] the first [source of Adam's power], was higher than [the power of her Son,[7] who is] the second [source of Adam's power], and the Shekinah], the higher [source of Adam's power], arose [into this World of Action] last,[8] and

[R-2] Jn 10:7
[R-2] Gen 2:10

---

[4]   **Mighty man** is a translation of אַיִל ' *(ayil)*, ***Strong's*** 352. See, **Lecture Notes for Verse 3** at Appendix #3, p *36*)

[5]   The ***Shekinah*** and ***Ze'ir Anpin***, the Mother and the Son of the God World of Emanation (*Atzilut*) are called ***Elohim***, ***God***, when they appear as a singularity. . . . (Footnote continued in Appendix #3, p *36*)

[6]   The Shekinah is the third of ten degrees of power called ***the ten Sefirot of the God World of Emanation (Atzilut)***. She is Jehovah's mate and her descriptive personality is ***Mother***. She is the first of Adam's two sources of power.

[7]   The Shekinah's Son is the single descriptive personality of the fourth through the ninth of the ten degrees of power called ***the ten Sefirot of the God World of Emanation (Atzilut).*** He is the second of Adam's two sources of power.

[8]   This present world came into existence after Adam fell down from the World of Creation ***(Beriah)***. The Son (Ze'ir Anpin) of the God World of Emanation (Atzilut) fell also . . . . (Footnote continued in Appendix #3, p *36*).

The Prophecies Of Daniel According to Kabbalah, Chapter 8/ Footnoted Version

Adam, Unstoppable

4   I saw [Righteous Adam], the mighty man [who was the personality of Primordial Adam], the nonexistent one,[9] pushing forth into

(1)   The [emotional] sea [of the World of Forms (Yetzirah), [10] and into]

(2)   The hidden, dark place [of the unconscious mind of the female goats], and into

(3)   The desert [World of Creation (Beriah), where Adam is formed, and]

He was twisting together[11] with the [female goats, and] the whole living creature could not stand before [Righteous Adam], or deliver [themselves] out of his hand,[R-1] and [Righteous Adam] did whatever he wanted to do[R-2] [with the females goats],[12] and

[R-1] Gen 9:2
[R-2] Gen 6:1-2

---

[9]   Existence implies manifestation. ***Primordial Adam***, called ***the Ancient of Days*** in Daniel 7, is called ***the nonexistent one*** because he is not of this world. ... (Footnote continued in Appendix #4, p *39).*

[10]   The Astral Plane.

[11]   Incarnation.

[12]   Righteous Adam was marrying the daughters of Adam (man) (Gen 6:2), to become their higher mind, which worships Jehovah.

Two Males

5   As I [AM gave me the] understanding [of the vision], there it was! A male Goat and a company of female goats[13] who were collectively male,[14] and [Righteous Adam], the personality of the nonexistent one who comes from the region of the evening sun,[15] [who is] above the whole earth[en creature], had spiritual sexual intercourse with [the female goats that the Lizard formed from] the ground, and the male Goat [who had] the power of vision [from the brow energy center] between his eyes,[16] [saw what was happening, and]

A Large Lizard

6   [I saw] a large Lizard[17] rush towards [Righteous Adam], the personality [that] was standing by the river [that flows out of Eden and] he was enraged,[R-1] and he came as a husband[18] at [the female side[R-2] of Righteous Adam], the mighty man who had two sources of power, and

[R-1] Gen 4:5

---

[13]   The male Goat is the Man of Sin, the offspring of the Lizard and the female sheep, the humans who fornicate with the Lizard. Spiritual birth is of the mind. (Footnote continued in Appendix #5, p *42*).

[14]   The combined spiritual power of all of the female goats was equal to the spiritual power of the male Goat who was competing with Righteous Adam to control and be the king over the female goats.

[15]   The first rays of the rising sun are called **morning** because when they shine upon the spiritual darkness called **Night** (Gen 1:5) the hybrid soul called **evening** comes into existence. . . . (Footnote continued in Appendix #5, p *45).*

[16]   The Sixth energy center.

[17]   **Large Lizard** is a legitimate translation of Strong's 3581, the Hebrew word translated **of his** in verse 6. The word actually means **power** or **strength**. . . . (Footnote continued in Appendix #6 p *47*).

[18]   **This Lizard** is a spiritual being, as is Adam. All of mankind is spiritually female, physical males as well as physical females. Adam and the Lizard, two spiritual males . . . (Footnote continued in Appendix #6, p *47*).

The Prophecies Of Daniel According to Kabbalah, Chapter 8/ Footnoted Version

^{R-2} Gen 1:27

Adam's Power Broken

7   I saw [the Lizard come] near to [the female side[19] of Righteous Adam], the mighty man, [and] have spiritual sexual intercourse[20] with [his female] side, [and when the Lizard] struck [Righteous Adam], the mighty man, [by having spiritual sexual intercourse with his female side, Righteous Adam's] two power sources burst [apart],[21] and there was no strength in [Righteous Adam] to throw the personality of [the male Goat] down to the ground[22] and tread upon him,^R and there was no [spiritual source powerful enough] to snatch [Righteous Adam], the mighty man, [and his male] drop,[23] away from the spiritual hand[24] [of the Lizard], and

^R Mal 4:3

---

[19]   Elohim made Adam both male and female (Gen 1:27; 2:22).

[20]   Spiritual sexual intercourse is a union of mind which brings a third entity into existence.

[21]   Elohim, Adam's dual power source, broke up into the Mother and the Son. (See, also, Note #5.)

[22]   Fallen Adam did not have the strength to overthrow the personality of a female goat which had overthrown and replaced the personality of Righteous Adam.

[23]   Righteous Adam's primordial male reproductive force before it became a seed.

[24]   The male Goat is the spiritual hand of the Lizard, just like Righteous Adam is the spiritual hand of Jehovah.

Marrying the Females

8a   The male Goat vehemently twisted [together] with [Jehovah's gazelle,[25] who had Righteous Adam's nature],[26] in the same manner [that Righteous Adam twisted together with the female goats that had the Lizard's nature,[R] and

[R] Gen 6:1-2

A Bone Crunching Victory

8b   Daniel saw [in] I [AM's] vision, [that] the widow[ed Adam][27] became strong enough [to overcome] the great power [of the Lizard,[28] and he saw] the four [faces of Righteous Adam],[29] the Son [of God], ascend [from underneath the personality of the female goat] and replace the four [faces of fallen Adam], and [Daniel saw [Righteous Adam] crunch the spiritual bones [of the female goat] personality [of the Lizard] that had overthrown his male personality, and

---

[25]   *Gazelle* is a name of endearment for the Israel of God. (See, also, Lecture Notes for Verse #8 in Appendix #8, p *52*).

[26]   Righteous Adam has the nature of Jehovah.

[27]   The four types of nature found in the widowed Adam, i.e., Adam that is regenerated in a human, but not yet rejoined . . . . (Footnote continued in Appendix #8, p 51). (See, also, Note #5, and the Lecture Notes for Verse #8 in Appendix #8, p *52*).

[28]   The Lizard is stronger than Adam when he is cut off from his Mother. The Mother and the Son, together, . . . (Footnote continued in Appendix #8, p *51*).

[29]   The four aspects of the nature of Adam (Man), the Son of God. (See, Lecture Notes for Verse #8 in Appendix #8, p *52*).

A Seed Goes Forth

9   [Adam's male drop], the little united power,[30] went forth from the part of [Righteous Adam that was] united with [the Shekinah, Adam's Mother, and it] twisted [together with the human spirit], the superior [part of the widowed Adam], the gazelle [that Jehovah formed] in the desert [World of Creation (Beriah), and Primordial Adam],[R] the rising sun[31] [of the Third Day of Creation,[32] carried it] toward

[R] Dan 7:13

The Armies of Heaven

10   [The holy ones, and][33] it twisted together with the armies of heaven,[R-1] and they cast down some of the princes[34] of the armies of [the Lizard] to the ground,[R-1] and tread[R-2] upon them, and

[R-1] Rev 12:7
[R-2] Mal 4:3

---

[30]   *The little united power* is the seed that contains the blended DNA of Righteous Adam and the Shekinah, the third degree of power of the God World of Emanation (Atzilut).

[31]   The term *the rising sun* is rendered from the Hebrew word translated *first emanations* (morning) in Gen 1:8. (Footnote continued in Appendix #9, p *54*).

[32]   Life begins to appear on the Third Day of Creation.

[33]   The people of Israel who are sanctified and made holy through a relationship with the God of Israel. These are also called *saints*, or *sons of God*.

[34]   *Princes* in Scripture are usually archangels or other spiritual powers assigned to human beings. There are good and evil princes . . . . (Footnote continued in Appendix #10, p *56*).

Michael, the Prince

11   [Michael], the Prince[R] of the armies [of heaven] twisted [together with] the holy ones to raise up the continual sacrifice,[35] and [the armies of heaven] cast down the part of [the Lizard that was occupying] their dwelling places,[36] and

[R] Dan 12:1

The Atonement

12   The armies [of heaven] pushed forward from above to put the continual sacrifice in place for the rebels[R-1] [who became goats after] they cast the truth down[R-2] to the ground;

[R-1] Num 20:10
Ez 20:38
[R-2] Is 59:14

How Long

13   Then I heard [Righteous Adam], one Holy One,[37] speaking, and [Righteous Adam], the one who spoke, said to [Gabriel], another Holy One, [tell Daniel about] the vision, [tell him,] how long [it will take for]

(1)   The daily [sacrifice and]

(2)   The rebellion [that] stunned and devastated [Righteous Adam [R] to end, and]

---

[35]   Under the First Covenant, a continuous burnt sacrifice was required to purge the day-to-day sins of Israel. (See, Appendix #11, p *59*).

[36]   Physical bodies.

[37]   Righteous Adam and Gabriel, as well as the people of Israel, are called *holy ones* (see, Note #33), but only Righteous Adam (Gen 1:26) and Gabriel (Dan 9:21) are called, *man[kind]*, signifying that they are *complete* men, accurate reflections of the reality in Heaven.

Holy One is capitalized in verse 13 to distinguish between the mortal men of Israel who are called *holy* by faith, and the immortal Righteous Adam and Gabriel who are truly holy (without sin).

The Prophecies Of Daniel According to Kabbalah, Chapter 8/ Footnoted Version

(3) To give the holy ones, [Jehovah's] armies, [the power] to tread [the Lizard] under foot, and

^R Gen 3:17-19

14 [Gabriel] said to me, until the evening and the morning of the Second Day of Creation, [when the Shekinah descends into] the holy ones [to become the Keter, Chochmah and Binah, the upper] triad[38] [of the Son of Adam,^R the one who] makes [them] righteous,[39] and

^R Matt 9:28

15 It came to pass that when Daniel saw I [AM's] vision and sought after the meaning, there it was! A man [who] appeared [to be] a mighty warrior stood opposite him,[40] and

Adam Calls Gabriel

16 [Daniel] heard Adam's voice [coming from] the midst of the solitary, unmarried image [of the warrior],[41] calling him by name,^{R-1} saying, Gabriel make this foolish [sheep^{R-2} who is my] other self, understand the vision, and

^{R-1} Ex 35:30
^{R-2} Jn 10:3

18 I was stunned, [and] as [Gabriel] spoke with me I fell into a trance, and [Gabriel] had spiritual sexual intercourse with my earth[en] personality, [and] stood me upright, and

---

[38] Binah of the God World of Emanation (Atzilut) descends into Tiferet, where she blends with Chesed and Gevurah. After that Tiferet descends into Malchut .... (Footnote Continued in Appendix #14, p *67*).

[39] The Shekinah became Adam's righteousness when Jehovah breathed the breath of life into him. The Shekinah is Jehovah's mate. .... (Footnote continued in Appendix #14, p *67*).

[40] *The mighty warrior* is Gabriel, the Son of Adam, being formed in Daniel. Daniel is the mirror image of Gabriel.

[41] *Humanity, homo sapien man, Strong's #121*, is the visible image of *Adam, the spiritual man* called *mankind, Strong's # 120* ..... (Footnote continued in Appendix #16, p *71*).

A Vision About the End Times

17   [Gabriel] said to me, understand, son of Adam, [that] the vision [is about] the end times,[42] and

Cain's Rage

19   [Gabriel] said, look! I will tell you [what] shall come to pass at the appointed time of the end, [when] Elohim, your other self,[43] [shall put] an end [to Cain's] rage,[R] [and what will come to pass concerning]

[R] Gen 4:6

Elohim Divided

22   (1)   The large Lizard [that] burst [apart the Mother and the Son], the two powers [which were revealed through Righteous Adam] in the [lower] window of [creation where Leviathan], the fish [is], and

(2)   The Serpent [who] stood up four nations [in the World of Action (Asiyah)][44] below [to replace] the four [spiritual] kingdoms[45] [that exist, but] are not standing up [in the visible world yet,[R] and]

[R] Rev 17:12

---

[42]   The end of the age.

[43]   All earthen vessels are called, *goat*, initially, because they are born with the fallen mind called *Cain*. The earthen vessels of Israel, however, like Daniel .... (Footnote continued in Appendix #19, p *76*).

[44]   Babylon, Media-Persia, Greece and Rome.

[45]   The Kingdom of God, the Kingdom of Heaven, the Kingdom of the Seas and the Kingdom of the Earth. Each of these Kingdoms is a reflection .... (Footnote continued in Appendix #22, p *86*).

The Prophecies Of Daniel According to Kabbalah, Chapter 8/ Footnoted Version

The Mud King

21 (3) The king [who] looks like a man, but is formed from the mud [and is really] an hybrid deity [of the household of the Lizard] that has horns, a tail and the hind legs of a goat, and the great power between his two eyes is [Nimrod],[46] the first king, and

Adam Fallen

24a The large Lizard [that empowers the male Goat] shall be mighty, and [fallen Adam] shall not have the power to separate [himself from the male Goat, but

The Shekinah Is Sufficient

20 The Mother and the Son of the God World of Emanation (Atzilut)], the two sources of power of [Righteous Adam], the mighty man that you saw, are sufficient [to overthrow] the kings[47] who broke into pieces [when they fell down into this world], and

---

[46] Nimrod was the first king to be an incarnation of Righteous Adam after the Flood, but he turned evil and became a world tyrant. Saul was the second king.... (Footnote continued in Appendix #21, p *84*).

[47] These are the kings of the World of Points, the world that preceded the God World of Emanation (Atzilut). The power of these kings was not adequately balanced.... (Footnote continued in Appendix #20, p *78*).

Procreative Spiritual Power

23   In the end time, a king with [spiritual] procreative power[48] and the [spiritual] intelligence[49] to understand the mysteries of the Kingdom [of God],[50] shall stand up and complete the personalities of the rebels,[51] and

The Lizard Defeated

24b   [The Son of the God World of Emanation (Atzilut)] shall push forward [into the earth], and destroy [the Lizard, and Righteous Adam] shall make [the male Goat] a ruin[ous heap, and acquire] a large number of [the female goats, and

---

[48]   The Malchut of the world above carries the spiritual DNA of the higher world to the world that is being created below, and is found within Arikh Anpin of the lower world. (Footnote continued in Appendix #23, p *88*).

[49]   ***Spiritual intelligence*** is the potential to understand spiritual mysteries that the human mind is not capable of, and the foundation necessary . . . . (Footnote continued in Appendix #23, p *88*).

[50]   The Kingdom of God is the Malchut of the God World of Emanation (Atzilut) and spiritual Israel, the righteous nation which is its reflection in the earth.

[51]   Humanity is incomplete because physical males as well as physical females are spiritually female and male and female sides are required for completion. (See, also, Note #37)

The Prophecies Of Daniel According to Kabbalah, Chapter 8/ Footnoted Version

The Prince of Princes

25   The Shekinah, Jehovah's] intelligence from above, shall push forward into the heart [center [52] where Righteous Adam is, and they shall form] the mind of peace[53] from above, [which] shall twist together with the ruined [mind of] the counterfeit [Son of Adam],[54] and the Prince of princes shall stand up in the many [members of humanity, and] end the [reptilian] rebellion,[55] and

A Vision For the Future

26   The vision of the evening and the morning [of the Second Day of Creation] which was told to you is true, [but] the vision will not come to pass for many days, so [the understanding of it] will be locked up [until the time appointed for it to come to pass[56]]; and

Daniel's Sickness

27   Daniel was physically weak [for many] days [after Righteous Adam, Gabriel's] mate from above, stood up [in him, because] the wisdom of I [AM] is the creative process that

---

[52]   Christ, the foundation of the spiritual building that reaches into heaven, is built up in our heart, but the Shekinah who is in heaven, must come down to complete it.

[53]   The mind that agrees with God, thus making peace (Eph 2:15) (Reference continued in Appendix #25, *93*).

[54]   Lucifer is the counterfeit Son of Adam. Satan and Lucifer are not the same being. Satan is a spirit, Lucifer is a man, the offspring of Cain. The Son of Adam (the Son of Man) is the offspring of Adam.

[55]   The reptilians were created on the Fifth Day of Creation and mankind was created on the Sixth Day. Adam, mankind, is the final phase of Jehovah's creation. . . . (Footnote continued in Appendix #25, p *92*).

[56]   Since the understanding is set forth in his work, we know that ***the end times*** is now.

destroys the king[dom of darkness, and Daniel] did not understand the vision.[57]

---

[57] The creative process conceives the Son of Adam in the individual. After that, the wisdom of the Word of God nourishes him until he becomes mature enough . . . . (Footnote continued in Appendix #27, p *95*).

APPENDICES

LECTURE NOTES

Message # 831
A HISTORY OF ADAM
(Daniel, Chapter 8)

Part 1

Appendix - Verse 1

No Lecture Notes

Reference Scriptures for Verse 1

Dan 7:2

2 Daniel spake and said, I saw in my vision by night, and, behold, the four winds of the heaven strove upon the great sea.

KJV

Appendix - Verse 2

Footnotes

Footnote #2 – Continued

. . . . who makes communication between God and man possible. Righteous Adam is the only Mediator between God and man. Righteous Adam is called Christ Jesus in the New Testament (1 Tim 2:5)

Adam, who is in both heaven and earth through the mind that was given to him, is the channel through which Jehovah communicates with mankind. This channel is called *Mediator*. Adam is the only Mediator between God and man.

Adam is a spiritual man and a spiritual Mediator. Today he exists as the higher mind of spiritual Israel.

The invisible presence of God dwells within a man through the spiritual man called Adam

The Shekinah, the breath that Jehovah breathed into Adam, dwells within the spiritual man Adam. When the spiritual man, Adam, is present as the mind of a man, the Shekinah is dwelling in that man through the mind call *Adam*, and that man is called *a Son of Adam*, or *a Son of Man*.

Footnote #3 – Continued

. . . . associated with the first degree of power of the God World of Emanation, is higher than the will of any single human, or the collective will of all of humanity. Humans who are under Jehovah's authority are called *sheep*. (Ps 78:52, Jer 50:6)

Ezek 2:1

² AND HE SAID UNTO ME, SON OF MAN, STAND UPON THY FEET, AND I WILL SPEAK UNTO THEE.

KJV

The Prophecies Of Daniel According to Kabbalah, Chapter 8/ Lecture Notes (Part 1)

Dan 7:13

¹³ I SAW IN THE NIGHT VISIONS, AND, BEHOLD, ONE LIKE THE SON OF MAN CAME WITH THE CLOUDS OF HEAVEN, AND CAME TO THE ANCIENT OF DAYS, AND THEY BROUGHT HIM NEAR BEFORE HIM.

KJV

Luke 5:24

²⁴ BUT THAT YE MAY KNOW THAT THE SON OF MAN HATH POWER UPON EARTH TO FORGIVE SINS, (HE SAID UNTO THE SICK OF THE PALSY,) I SAY UNTO THEE, ARISE, AND TAKE UP THY COUCH, AND GO INTO THINE HOUSE.

KJV

Lecture Notes for Verse 2

² AND I SAW IN A VISION; AND IT CAME TO PASS, WHEN I SAW, THAT I WAS AT SHUSHAN IN THE PALACE, WHICH IS IN THE PROVINCE OF ELAM; AND I SAW IN A VISION, AND I WAS BY THE RIVER OF ULAI.

KJV

I saw house (prefix bet) vision to be (it came to pass) building (prefix bet) saw I(AM) house (prefix bet) Messiah (Shushan=lily) palace which hidden (Elam) judgeship/jurisdiction I saw (province) vision I(AM) was above (by) river foolish [shepherd] (Ulai)

Shushan = lily = Messiah = Righteous Adam

Song 2:2

² AS THE **LILY** AMONG THORNS, SO IS MY LOVE AMONG THE DAUGHTERS.

KJV

The Prophecies Of Daniel According to Kabbalah, Chapter 8/ Lecture Notes (Part 1)

I saw house vision to be building saw I(AM) house Messiah palace which hidden legal authority (Ulai=judgeship/jurisdiction) I saw vision I(AM) was above foolish [shepherd]

OT:196 - Ulai
195. אוּלַי **'ûlay**: A proper noun designating **Ulai** (Dan 8:2,16).

Dan. 8:2,16.

SAME LETTERS, DIFFERENT VOWELS

196. אֱוִלִי **(R)wiliy**: An adverb meaning foolish. It describes **a foolish shepherd** (Zech 11:15) who does not care for the sheep but rather destroys them.

(from The Complete Word Study Dictionary: Old Testament Copyright © 2003 by AMG Publishers. All rights reserved.)

I saw a vision [of a] building, [and] the building [that] I saw was the hidden palace of Messiah, the house[hold] of I (AM), [and] I saw in the vision that the legal authority of I (AM) was above [the legal authority] of the foolish [shepherd]

2   I saw a vision [of a] building, [and] the building [that] I saw was the hidden palace of Righteous Adam, the house[hold] of I [AM], [and] I saw in the vision that the legal authority of I [AM] was above [the legal authority] of the foolish [shepherd] , and (ATB)

Reference Scriptures for Verse 2

1 Kings 8:20

20 And the Lord hath performed his word that he spake, and I am risen up in the room of David my father, and sit on the throne of Israel, as the Lord promised, and have built an house for the name of the Lord God of Israel.
KJV

The Prophecies Of Daniel According to Kabbalah, Chapter 8/ Lecture
Notes (Part 1)

Zech 11:15

15 And the Lord said unto me, Take unto thee yet the instruments of a foolish shepherd.

KJV

The Prophecies Of Daniel According to Kabbalah, Chapter 8/ Lecture Notes (Part 1)

Appendix - Verse 3

Footnotes

Footnote #5 - Continued

Elohim is the power behind Adam, and the source of his designation, ***Son of God.***

Footnote #8 - Continued

.... but the Mother returned to the God World of Emanation (Atzilut). That singularity of their power burst apart when the male Goat of verse 7 attacked Adam who was still innocent of a knowledge of evil. The Son of the God World of Emanation (Atzilut) who was attached to innocent Adam, fell with him, but the Mother who was attached to the Father above, did not fall. So the Son entered into this World of Action (Asiyah) first because he fell with Adam, but the Mother will come into existence when the Lord Jesus Christ, the garment that clothes Elohim, appears for the second time.

Lecture Notes for Verse 3

> ³ THEN I LIFTED UP MINE EYES, AND SAW, AND, BEHOLD, THERE STOOD BEFORE THE RIVER A RAM WHICH HAD TWO HORNS: AND THE TWO HORNS WERE HIGH; BUT ONE WAS HIGHER THAN THE OTHER, AND THE HIGHER CAME UP LAST.
>
> **KJV**

Lifted up eyes saw there it was a mighty man (ram) [who was] the doorway [to the spiritual world of God] stood personality (before) river which had two hours (horns) high first (but one) then the second (other) the higher ascended last

The Prophecies Of Daniel According to Kabbalah, Chapter 8/ Lecture Notes (Part 1)

OT:352 - ram

352. אַיִל 'ayil:

    I. A masculine noun meaning ram. It is used in general of the **rams** of sacrifice, the most famous one being the ram God Himself provided in place of Isaac (Gen 22:13).

    II. A masculine noun indicating a gatepost or lintel. It refers to **doorposts** (1 Kings 6:31). It is translated as side pillars as well (NASB, Ezek 40:9,10,16).

    III. A masculine noun meaning leader or **mighty man**, i.e., a strong pillar or post for others to look to. It has this meaning many times. The leaders or mighty men in Moab are described figuratively with this word. It describes the leading men of Israel (2 Kings 24:15) or of the nations (Ps 58:1[2]).

    IV. A masculine noun referring to an oak tree or terebinth tree. This sacred fertility tree was associated with pagan worship (Isa 1:29; 57:5). God's faithful people should rather be oaks of righteousness (NASB, Isa 61:3). It can refer to especially strong or huge trees (Ezek 31:14).

(from The Complete Word Study Dictionary: Old Testament Copyright © 2003 by AMG Publishers. All rights reserved.)

Lifted up eyes saw there it was a mighty man [who was] the doorway [to the spiritual world of God] stood personality river which had two powers high first then the second the higher ascended last

I lifted up eyes and there he was! I saw a mighty man, [even] the personality [who was] the doorway to the river [that flows out of Eden, and] he stood two powers high first then the second the higher ascended last

Gen 2:10

¹⁰ **AND A RIVER WENT OUT OF EDEN** TO WATER THE GARDEN; AND FROM THENCE IT WAS PARTED, AND BECAME INTO FOUR HEADS.

KJV

3   I lifted up eyes and there he was! I saw [Righteous Adam], a mighty man [whose] personality [was] the doorway [to the spiritual world of God, and] he was standing by the river [that flows out of Eden, and] he had two sources of power, and the first [source of power] was higher than the second [source of power], and] the higher [source of power] arose [into this world] last, and **(ATB)**

John 10:9

⁹ **I AM THE DOOR**: BY ME IF ANY MAN ENTER IN, HE SHALL BE SAVED, AND SHALL GO IN AND OUT, AND FIND PASTURE.

KJV

COMMENT: the two sources of power are the Shekinah and the Son

Reference Scriptures for Verse 3

John 10:7

7 Then said Jesus unto them again, Verily, verily, I say unto you, I am the door of the sheep.

KJV

Gen 2:10

10 And a river went out of Eden to water the garden; and from thence it was parted, and became into four heads.

KJV

Appendix - Verse 4

Footnotes

Footnote #9 - Continued

Primordial Adam is the spiritual glue that holds the creation together:

Acts 17:28

> 28 FOR IN HIM WE LIVE, AND MOVE, AND HAVE OUR BEING; AS CERTAIN ALSO OF YOUR OWN POETS HAVE SAID, FOR WE ARE ALSO HIS OFFSPRING.
>
> **KJV**

Primordial Adam did not exist in this World of Action (Asiyah) from its inception, which took place after Adam fell, but he will come into existence here when the Lord Jesus Christ appears for the second time.

Jesus is to Primordial Adam as Joseph was to Pharaoh. The Lord Jesus Christ is Primordial Adam's viceroy and the spiritual garment that reveals him in this World of Action.

Lecture Notes for Verse 4

> 4 I SAW THE RAM PUSHING WESTWARD, AND NORTHWARD, AND SOUTHWARD; SO THAT NO BEASTS MIGHT STAND BEFORE HIM, NEITHER WAS THERE ANY THAT COULD DELIVER OUT OF HIS HAND; BUT HE DID ACCORDING TO HIS WILL, AND BECAME GREAT.
>
> **KJV**

I saw the mighty man pushing forth into the [emotional] sea [of Yetzirah] (westward), the hidden dark place [of the unconscious mind] (northward), and into the desert [of Beriah] (southward) whole (so that) living thing (beasts) no stand before him the nonexistent one (neither was there any) to deliver out of his hand and he did what he wanted to do (according to his will) and became great

I saw the mighty man pushing forth into the [emotional] sea [of Yetzirah], the hidden dark place [of the unconscious mind], and into the desert [of Beriah] whole living thing no stand the nonexistent one to deliver out of his hand and he did what he wanted to do and became great

I saw the mighty man pushing forth into the [emotional] sea [of Yetzirah, and into] the hidden, dark place [of the unconscious mind], and into the desert [of Beriah where Adam is formed, and] the whole living creature [that had been created up to the point of the fifth day] could not stand before the nonexistent one, or deliver [themselves] out of his hand, and he did all that he wanted to do, and he twisted together

Gen 6:1-2

¹ AND IT CAME TO PASS, WHEN MEN BEGAN TO MULTIPLY ON THE FACE OF THE EARTH, AND DAUGHTERS WERE BORN UNTO THEM,

² THAT THE SONS OF GOD SAW THE DAUGHTERS OF MEN THAT THEY WERE FAIR; AND THEY TOOK THEM WIVES OF ALL WHICH THEY CHOSE.

KJV

4 **I saw a mighty man, [Righteous Adam, the personality of] the nonexistent one, pushing forth into the [emotional] sea [of Yetzirah,, and into] the hidden, dark place [of Righteous Adam's unconscious mind], and into the desert [of Beriah, the World of Creation, where Adam is formed, and] he twisted together with the [spiritual females of creation, and] the whole living creature could not stand before [Righteous Adam], or deliver [themselves] out of his hand, and [Righteous Adam] did everything that he wanted to do [with the spiritual females of creation], and (ATB)**

The Prophecies Of Daniel According to Kabbalah, Chapter 8/ Lecture Notes (Part 1)

Reference Scriptures for Verse 4

Gen 9:2

2 And the fear of you and the dread of you shall be upon every beast of the earth, and upon every fowl of the air, upon all that moveth upon the earth, and upon all the fishes of the sea; into your hand are they delivered.

KJV

Gen 6:1-2

1 And it came to pass, when men began to multiply on the face of the earth, and daughters were born unto them,

2 That the sons of God saw the daughters of men that they were fair; and they took them wives of all which they chose.

KJV

Appendix - Verse 5

Footnotes

Footnote #13 – Continued

The Man of Sin is born in the humans who fornicate with the Lizard as a new mind with the nature of the Lizard.

Background

The wife of the spiritual man, Adam, ***mankind***, committed adultery with the Snake, and Adam, ***mankind***, agreed with the transgression (Gen 3:6), so the judgment fell upon Adam (Gen 3:17-19), as well as his wife (Gen 3:16) and the Snake (Gen 3:14-15), a reptilian created on the Fifth Day of Creation.

Gen 3:6

> [6] AND WHEN THE WOMAN SAW THAT THE TREE WAS GOOD FOR FOOD, AND THAT IT WAS PLEASANT TO THE EYES, AND A TREE TO BE DESIRED TO MAKE ONE WISE, SHE TOOK OF THE FRUIT THEREOF, AND DID EAT, AND GAVE ALSO UNTO HER HUSBAND WITH HER; AND HE DID EAT.

KJV

Gen 3:17-19

> [17] AND UNTO ADAM HE SAID, BECAUSE THOU HAST HEARKENED UNTO THE VOICE OF THY WIFE, AND HAST EATEN OF THE TREE, OF WHICH I COMMANDED THEE, SAYING, THOU SHALT NOT EAT OF IT: CURSED IS THE GROUND FOR THY SAKE; IN SORROW SHALT THOU EAT OF IT ALL THE DAYS OF THY LIFE;
>
> [18] THORNS ALSO AND THISTLES SHALL IT BRING FORTH TO THEE; AND THOU SHALT EAT THE HERB OF THE FIELD;

[19] IN THE SWEAT OF THY FACE SHALT THOU EAT BREAD, TILL THOU RETURN UNTO THE GROUND; FOR OUT OF IT WAST THOU TAKEN: FOR DUST THOU ART, AND UNTO DUST SHALT THOU RETURN.

KJV

Gen 3:16

[16] UNTO THE WOMAN HE SAID, I WILL GREATLY MULTIPLY THY SORROW AND THY CONCEPTION; IN SORROW THOU SHALT BRING FORTH CHILDREN; AND THY DESIRE SHALL BE TO THY HUSBAND, AND HE SHALL RULE OVER THEE.

KJV

Gen 3:14-15

[14] AND THE LORD GOD SAID UNTO THE SERPENT, BECAUSE THOU HAST DONE THIS, THOU ART CURSED ABOVE ALL CATTLE, AND ABOVE EVERY BEAST OF THE FIELD; UPON THY BELLY SHALT THOU GO, AND DUST SHALT THOU EAT ALL THE DAYS OF THY LIFE:

[15] AND I WILL PUT ENMITY BETWEEN THEE AND THE WOMAN, AND BETWEEN THY SEED AND HER SEED; IT SHALL BRUISE THY HEAD, AND THOU SHALT BRUISE HIS HEEL.

KJV

The adulterous Woman appeared in the lower world as a duality, the earthen part of her as a herd of spiritual female goats, and the spiritual part of her as an invisible spiritual entity, a fallen angel who desired to complete herself in the lower world. So she married as many of the female goats, her other self, as she could, and became their intelligent mind.

All of the spiritual female goats that the Woman married became spiritual male goats. The collective personal name of the herd of spiritual goats is ***Cain***, but they are known today as ***humanity***. The spiritual goats that have an intelligent spiritual mind are male, and the spiritual goats who do not have an intelligent spiritual mind are female.

So, humanity is the fallen Woman in another form.

After that, the Snake became the unconscious mind of the male goats by marrying them, and the spiritual intelligent mind that they received from the Woman increased into an hybrid intellectual mind called **Leviathan.**

But the Snake that Elohim created on the Fifth Day of Creation did not blend fully with the Sixth Day consciousness of the intellectual goats. The reptilian continues to exist both independently, outside of the herd of goats as well as inside of them, The Snake is called a *Lizard* in Daniel 8, because he inhabits the spiritual seawaters of the World of Forms (Yetzirah), as well as the dry land of the World of Action (Asiyah).

This herd of spiritual goats, both the females and the males, that are protected by the Lizard, is Adam's mate in the World of Action (Asiyah), and the spiritual man, Adam, *mankind,* is the help that Jehovah provided for the fallen Woman, called *humanity*, who became a herd of spiritual goats.

Adam and the Lizard have been at war to determine who is the legitimate heir to, and king of the earthen vessels called *goats* (*sheep* when Adam's mind overtakes them), that is, who will dominate Cain, the reptilian hybrid.

There are now two spiritual bloodlines within the earthen vessels of *humanity*:

Cain, the reptilian offspring of the adulteress and the Snake, and *Abel*, the offspring of Elohim and Righteous Adam.

The Lizard mates with Cain, who births ***Lucifer, the Man of Sin,*** and Righteous Adam mates with Abel who births ***the Son of Adam (the Son of Man).***

Gen 2:18

¹⁸ AND THE LORD GOD SAID, IT IS NOT GOOD THAT THE MAN SHOULD BE ALONE; I WILL MAKE HIM AN HELP MEET FOR HIM.

KJV

Genesis 2:18 - AT: *And Jehovah Elohim said, it is not good for Adam, mankind, to be alone, I will make a mate for him to assist (ATB)*

Footnote #15 - Continued

The region of the evening sun is any place where the Sun of Righteousness (Mal 4:2) enlightens the ignorant dark Night of the soul. (See, Alternate Translation of Gen 1:7-8, in the Lecture Notes for Verse 14, at Appendix #14, p 67)

Lecture Notes for Verse 5

⁵ AND AS I WAS CONSIDERING, BEHOLD, AN HE GOAT CAME FROM THE WEST ON THE FACE OF THE WHOLE EARTH, AND TOUCHED NOT THE GROUND: AND THE GOAT HAD A NOTABLE HORN BETWEEN HIS EYES.

KJV

And as I to be intelligence/understanding (considering) there it was (behold) a male goat (6842) a company of female goats who are collectively male (5795) (an he goat) came the part of (from) the region of the evening sun (West) above (on) personality (the face of) all earth nonexistent one (and not) to lie with a women (touched) the ground male goat's power (horn) striking appearance/vision (notable) between his eyes

The Prophecies Of Daniel According to Kabbalah, Chapter 8/ Lecture Notes (Part 1)

And as I to be intelligence/understanding there it was a male goat a company of female goats who are collectively male came the part of the region of the evening sun above personality all earth nonexistent one to lie with a women the ground male goat's power striking appearance/vision between his eyes

And as I was understanding [the vision]: There it was! A male goat and a company of female goats who were collectively male, and the personality of the nonexistent one who comes from the region of the evening sun [which is] above the whole earth[en creation] had spiritual sexual intercourse with the ground, and the male goat had the power of vision [in his world and in the world of the non-existent one] and

Deut 6:8
> [8] AND THOU SHALT BIND THEM FOR A SIGN UPON THINE HAND, AND THEY SHALL BE **AS FRONTLETS BETWEEN THINE EYES.**
> KJV

COMMENT: the company of female goats were formed from the ground, which is the dust mixed with the moisture of the abyss. The male goat is the fetus of the Cainites impregnated by the lizard.

The company of female goats is Cain, the male goat is the company of Cainites who are possessed by the Woman.

5   [And] as I [AM gave me] understanding [of the vision], there it was! A male goat and a company of female goats who were collectively male, and [Righteous Adam], the personality of the nonexistent one who comes from the region of the evening sun, [who is] above the whole earth[en creature], had spiritual sexual intercourse with [the female goats who were formed from] the ground, and the male goat [who had] the power of vision [from the brow energy center] between the eyes, [saw what was happening, and] (ATB)

The Prophecies Of Daniel According to Kabbalah, Chapter 8/ Lecture Notes (Part 1)

Appendix - Verse 6

Footnotes

Footnote #17 – Continued

The King James translators most likely did not know what to do with that word in the context of verse 6, so they marginalized it down to *of his*.

The Hebrew word translated **Lizard** also means **reptilian**, and, therefore, may be interchanged with *snake* or *serpent*.

Footnote #18 - Continued

... were both incarnating in as many human beings as they were able to, Adam as the mind of God and the Lizard as the amoral mind of Cain.

The Lizard not only broke Adam's power to incarnate the mind of God in humanity, he made a woman out of Righteous Adam.

When that happened, all the humans who were worshipping Jehovah through Righteous Adam, the only Mediator between God and man, were overtaken by the Lizard who changed the image of God in their mind to the image of Cain.

Rom 1:23

[23] AND CHANGED THE GLORY OF THE UNCORRUPTIBLE GOD INTO AN IMAGE MADE LIKE TO CORRUPTIBLE MAN, AND TO BIRDS, AND FOURFOOTED BEASTS, AND CREEPING THINGS.

KJV

Lecture Notes For Verse 6

[6] AND HE CAME TO THE RAM THAT HAD TWO HORNS, WHICH I HAD THERE SEEN STANDING BEFORE

THE RIVER, AND RAN UNTO HIM IN THE FURY OF HIS POWER.

KJV

Came to the mighty man (ram) master/husband/owner (that had) (two not in the Hebrew) power sources (horns) which saw (I had there) to stand (seen) personality (standing) a river (before the) to rush (and river) towards (ran into) of anger (fury) a large lizard (of his)

COMMENT: I previously thought that the Woman married to the Snake became a new entity, the combined woman and snake, but apparently not. Cain is the new entity. He is the offspring of the Woman formed as an animal, with the nature of the Snake and the woman is his amoral mind. The fifth day creations that seduced her remain reptilian, as we see in verse six.

6   [I saw] a large lizard rush towards [Righteous Adam], the personality [that] was standing by the river [that flows out of Eden, and] he was enraged, and he came to [the female side of Righteous Adam], the mighty man who had two sources of power, as a husband, and (ATB)

Reference Scriptures for Verse 6

Gen 4:5

5 But unto Cain and to his offering he had not respect. And Cain was very wroth, and his countenance fell.

KJV

Gen 1:27

27 So God created man in his own image, in the image of God created he him; male and female created he them.

KJV

The Prophecies Of Daniel According to Kabbalah, Chapter 8/ Lecture Notes (Part 1)

Appendix - Verse 7

Lecture Notes For Verse #7

⁷ AND I SAW HIM COME CLOSE UNTO THE RAM, AND HE WAS MOVED WITH CHOLER AGAINST HIM, AND SMOTE THE RAM, AND BRAKE HIS TWO HORNS: AND THERE WAS NO POWER IN THE RAM TO STAND BEFORE HIM, BUT HE CAST HIM DOWN TO THE GROUND, AND STAMPED UPON HIM: AND THERE WAS NONE THAT COULD DELIVER THE RAM OUT OF HIS HAND.

KJV

I saw have spiritual sexual intercourse (touch=come) with [the female] side (close unto) the mighty man (ram) [and his male] drop (and he was moved with choler =trickle=drop] [and he came] near (against) smote the mighty man (ram) burst [apart] two power sources (horns) no was power in the mighty man (ran) personality (before him) to throw down (but he cast him down to) the ground tread upon him (stamped upon him) none was to snatch away (that could deliver) the mighty man (ram) spiritual (prefix mem) hand

Mal 4:3

³ AND **YE SHALL TREAD DOWN THE WICKED**; FOR THEY SHALL BE ASHES UNDER THE SOLES OF YOUR FEET IN THE DAY THAT I SHALL DO THIS, SAITH THE LORD OF HOSTS.

KJV

7   I saw [the lizard come] near to [the female side of Righteous Adam], the mighty man, [and] have spiritual sexual intercourse with [his female] side, [and when the lizard] struck [Righteous Adam], the mighty man, [by having spiritual sexual intercourse with his female side, Righteous Adam's] two power sources burst [apart], and there was no strength in [Righteous Adam], the mighty man, to throw the personality of [the lizard] down to the ground and tread upon him, and there was no [spiritual source

The Prophecies Of Daniel According to Kabbalah, Chapter 8/ Lecture
Notes (Part 1)

powerful enough] to snatch [Righteous Adam], the mighty man, [and his male] drop, away from the spiritual hand [of the lizard], and (ATB)

Reference Scriptures for Verse 7

Mal 4:3

3 And ye shall tread down the wicked; for they shall be ashes under the soles of your feet in the day that I shall do this, saith the Lord of hosts.

KJV

Appendix - Verse 8

Footnotes

Footnote #27 - Continued

... to the God World of Emanation (Atzilut) through a union with his Mother.

> Widowed Adam:
>
> **Ezek 1:10**
>
> > [10] AS FOR THE LIKENESS OF THEIR FACES, THEY FOUR HAD THE FACE OF A MAN, AND THE FACE OF A LION, ON THE RIGHT SIDE: AND THEY FOUR HAD **THE FACE OF AN OX** ON THE LEFT SIDE; THEY FOUR ALSO HAD THE FACE OF AN EAGLE.
>
> **KJV**

Footnote #28 - Continued

.... are *Elohim, God*, and the man that Elohim is revealed through is called *a Son of God*, if he follows after that Spirit. Neither the Mother nor the Son, alone, is God.

Footnote #29 - Continued

Abel is Adam regenerated in a human, but still cut off from his Mother and from Elohim, God.

Adam, the Son of God:

Ezek 10:14

¹⁴ AND EVERY ONE HAD FOUR FACES: THE FIRST FACE WAS THE **FACE OF A CHERUB**, AND THE SECOND FACE WAS THE FACE OF A MAN, AND THE THIRD THE FACE OF A LION, AND THE FOURTH THE FACE OF AN EAGLE.

KJV

Lecture Notes For Verse 8

Dan 8:8

^{8A} THEREFORE THE HE GOAT WAXED VERY GREAT:

KJV

^{8a} And the he goat and the she goats who formed a collective male twisted [together] (waxed great) vehemently (3966) in the same manner (3704) (very) [that Righteous Adam had twisted together with the she goats formed from the ground]

8a **The male goat vehemently twisted [together] with [the gazelle, who had Righteous Adam's nature], in the same manner [that Righteous Adam twisted together with the female goats that formed a collective male goat, who had the Lizard's nature], (ATB)**

^{8B} AND WHEN HE WAS STRONG, THE GREAT HORN WAS BROKEN; AND FOR IT CAME UP FOUR NOTABLE ONES TOWARD THE FOUR WINDS OF HEAVEN.

KJV

But when [Righteous Adam] was strong enough to crunch the bones (was broken) [of the lizard] power (horn) great ascended (and it came

The Prophecies Of Daniel According to Kabbalah, Chapter 8/ Lecture Notes (Part 1)

up) vision (plural in English, but singular in Hebrew) four in place of (for) widow (prefix lamed) four spirits (winds) heaven

But when [Righteous Adam] was strong enough to crunch the bones [of the lizard] power great ascended vision four in place of widow four spirits the Son (heaven)

8b   But when [Righteous Adam] was strong enough [to overcome] the great power [of the Lizard, Daniel, saw in] the vision [that came from I AM], the four spirits of the Son [of Adam] ascend [from underneath the personality of the female goat] and replace the four [spirits of] the widow[ed Adam], and I saw [Righteous Adam] crunch the bones [of the female personality [of the collective male Goat] which had overthrown his male personality, and] (ATB)

Reference Scriptures for Verse 8

<u>Gen 6:1-2</u>

1 And it came to pass, when men began to multiply on the face of the earth, and daughters were born unto them,

2 That the sons of God saw the daughters of men that they were fair; and they took them wives of all which they chose.

KJV

The Prophecies Of Daniel According to Kabbalah, Chapter 8/ Lecture Notes (Part 1)

Appendix - Verse 9

Footnotes

Footnote #31 - Continued

The little united power, the male seed of Righteous Adam, rescued the human spirit (the residue in fallen Adam of the breath that Jehovah breathed into him), by uniting with it to empower its regeneration, which is the experience of the Third Day of Creation. See, also, Verse 14, p 67.

Matt 19:28

[28] AND JESUS SAID UNTO THEM, VERILY I SAY UNTO YOU, THAT YE WHICH HAVE FOLLOWED ME, IN THE REGENERATION WHEN THE SON OF MAN SHALL SIT IN THE THRONE OF HIS GLORY, YE ALSO SHALL SIT UPON TWELVE THRONES, JUDGING THE TWELVE TRIBES OF ISRAEL

KJV

Lecture Notes For Verse 9

[9] AND OUT OF ONE OF THEM CAME FORTH A LITTLE HORN, WHICH WAXED EXCEEDING GREAT, TOWARD THE SOUTH, AND TOWARD THE EAST, AND TOWARD THE PLEASANT LAND.

KJV

And a part of (out of) [Adam, who was] united (one) with [the Shekinah again] went forth (came forth) a power (horn) united (a=one) little twisted (which waxed great) superior (exceeding) towards the desert (south) toward the sunrise (east) toward splendor/gazelle (pleasant)

And a part of [Adam, who was] united with [the Shekinah again] went forth a power united little twisted superior towards the desert toward the sunrise toward splendor/gazelle

The Prophecies Of Daniel According to Kabbalah, Chapter 8/ Lecture Notes (Part 1)

Song 2:9

⁹ MY BELOVED IS LIKE A **GAZELLE** OR A YOUNG HART; BEHOLD, HE STANDS BEHIND OUR WALL, GAZING IN AT THE WINDOWS, LOOKING THROUGH THE LATTICE.

KJV

Soncino Zohar, Bereshith, Section 1, Page 4a

Who among you awaited every day the light that shall break forth what time the King shall visit his beloved **gazelle**, when He will be glorified and called King by all the kings of the world?

9   A little united power went forth from the part of [Righteous Adam that was] united with [the Shekinah, and it] twisted [together with the human spirit], the superior [part of Adam], the gazelle [that Jehovah formed] in the desert [World of Creation, and carried her] toward [Primordial Adam], the rising sun [of the Third Day of Creation], and (ATB)

Reference Scriptures for Verse 9

Dan 7:13

13 I saw in the night visions, and, behold, one like the Son of man came with the clouds of heaven, and came to the Ancient of days, and they brought him near before him.

KJV

Appendix - Verse 10

Footnotes

Footnote #34 - Continued

The people that these princes reveal themselves through are called *kings*.

Dan 10:13

> [13] BUT THE PRINCE OF THE KINGDOM OF PERSIA WITHSTOOD ME ONE AND TWENTY DAYS: BUT, LO, **MICHAEL, ONE OF THE CHIEF PRINCES**, CAME TO HELP ME; AND I REMAINED THERE WITH THE KINGS OF PERSIA.

KJV

Dan 10:21

> [21] BUT I WILL SHEW THEE THAT WHICH IS NOTED IN THE SCRIPTURE OF TRUTH: AND THERE IS NONE THAT HOLDETH WITH ME IN THESE THINGS, BUT **MICHAEL YOUR PRINCE**.

KJV

Dan 12:1

> [12] AND AT THAT TIME SHALL **MICHAEL** STAND UP, **THE GREAT PRINCE** WHICH STANDETH FOR THE CHILDREN OF THY PEOPLE: AND THERE SHALL BE A TIME OF TROUBLE, SUCH AS NEVER WAS SINCE THERE WAS A NATION EVEN TO THAT SAME TIME: AND AT THAT TIME THY PEOPLE SHALL BE DELIVERED, EVERY ONE THAT SHALL BE FOUND WRITTEN IN THE BOOK.

KJV

Ezek 38:3

³ AND SAY, THUS SAITH THE LORD GOD; BEHOLD I AM AGAINST THEE, O GOG, **THE CHIEF PRINCE OF MESHECH AND TUBAL**:

KJV

Lecture Notes For Verse 10

¹⁰ AND IT WAXED GREAT, EVEN TO THE HOST OF HEAVEN; AND IT CAST DOWN SOME OF THE HOST AND OF THE STARS TO THE GROUND, AND STAMPED UPON THEM.

KJV

And twisted together (waxed great) to the degree that (to) armies (host) heaven cast down ground a part of (of) armies a part of (and of) the stars tred upon them

And twisted together to the degree that armies heaven cast down ground a part of armies a part of the stars tred upon them

10   Twisted together [with Adam, Jehovah's gazelle] to the degree that the armies of heaven cast down some of the stars of the armies of [the male Goat] to the ground, and tread upon them, and (ATB)

Reference Scriptures for Verse 10

Rev 12:7

7 And there was war in heaven: Michael and his angels fought against the dragon; and the dragon fought and his angels,

KJV

The Prophecies Of Daniel According to Kabbalah, Chapter 8/ Lecture
Notes (Part 1)

<u>Mal 4:3</u>

3 And ye shall tread down the wicked; for they shall be ashes under the soles of your feet in the day that I shall do this, saith the Lord of hosts.

KJV

The Prophecies Of Daniel According to Kabbalah, Chapter 8/ Lecture Notes (Part 1)

Appendix - Verse 11

Lecture Notes for Verse 11

> ¹¹ YEA, HE MAGNIFIED HIMSELF EVEN TO THE PRINCE OF THE HOST, AND BY HIM THE DAILY SACRIFICE WAS TAKEN AWAY, AND THE PLACE OF HIS SANCTUARY WAS CAST DOWN.
>
> **KJV**

To the degree (even to) the Prince of the armies (host) twisted [together with] (magnified) a part of (and by him) raised up (was taken away) the continual sacrifice (daily) cast down place dwelling places/foundation (place of) holy ones (sanctuaries)

To the degree the Prince of the armies twisted [together with] a part of raised up the continual sacrifice cast down place dwelling places/foundation holy ones

Num 28:2-6

> ² COMMAND THE CHILDREN OF ISRAEL, AND SAY UNTO THEM, MY OFFERING, AND MY BREAD FOR MY SACRIFICES MADE BY FIRE, FOR A SWEET SAVOUR UNTO ME, SHALL YE OBSERVE TO OFFER UNTO ME IN THEIR DUE SEASON.
>
> ³ AND THOU SHALT SAY UNTO THEM, THIS IS THE OFFERING MADE BY FIRE WHICH YE SHALL OFFER UNTO THE LORD ; TWO LAMBS OF THE FIRST YEAR WITHOUT SPOT DAY BY DAY, FOR A CONTINUAL BURNT OFFERING.
>
> ⁴ THE ONE LAMB SHALT THOU OFFER IN THE MORNING, AND THE OTHER LAMB SHALT THOU OFFER AT EVEN;
>
> ⁵ AND A TENTH PART OF AN EPHAH OF FLOUR FOR A MEAT OFFERING, MINGLED WITH THE FOURTH PART OF AN HIN OF BEATEN OIL.

⁶ IT IS A CONTINUAL BURNT OFFERING, WHICH WAS ORDAINED IN MOUNT SINAI FOR A SWEET SAVOUR, A SACRIFICE MADE BY FIRE UNTO THE LORD.
KJV

11 To the degree that the Prince of the armies [of heaven] twisted [together with the human spirit, the superior] part [of Adam, Jehovah's gazelle], to raise up the continual sacrifice, and cast down [the male personality of the Goat who was occupying] the dwelling places of the holy ones. (ATB)

Reference Scriptures for Verse 11

Dan 12:1

1 And at that time shall Michael stand up, the great prince which standeth for the children of thy people: and there shall be a time of trouble, such as never was since there was a nation even to that same time: and at that time thy people shall be delivered, every one that shall be found written in the book
KJV

Appendix - Verse 12

Lecture Notes For Verse 12

¹² AND AN HOST WAS GIVEN HIM AGAINST THE DAILY SACRIFICE BY REASON OF TRANSGRESSION, AND IT CAST DOWN THE TRUTH TO THE GROUND; AND IT PRACTISED, AND PROSPERED.
KJV

Army (host) given above (against) continual sacrifice (daily) rebellion (by reason of transgression) cast down truth ground made (practiced) to push forward (prospered)

Army given above continual sacrifice rebellion cast down truth ground made to push forward

OT:8548 –continual sacrifice (da9ly)

<u>OT:8548</u> תָּמִיד **tamiyd** (taw-meed'); from an unused root meaning to stretch; properly, **continuance** (as indefinite extension); but used only (attributively as adjective) constant (or adverbially, constantly); ellipt. the regular (daily) sacrifice:

KJV - alway (-s), continual (employment, -ly), daily, ([n-]) ever (-more), perpetual.

OT:2077 – daily sacrifice

<u>OT:2077</u> זֶבַח **zebach** (zeh'-bakh); from <u>OT:2076</u>; properly, **a slaughter**, i.e. the flesh of an animal; by implication, a sacrifice (the victim or the act):

KJV - offer (-ing), sacrifice.

(Biblesoft's New Exhaustive Strong's Numbers and Concordance with Expanded Greek-Hebrew Dictionary. Copyright © 1994, 2003, 2006 Biblesoft, Inc. and International Bible Translators, Inc.)

12   And the armies [of heaven] pushed forward from above to put the continual sacrifice in place for the rebels [who] cast the truth down to the ground, (ATB)

Reference Scriptures for Verse 12

Num 20:10

10 And Moses and Aaron gathered the congregation together before the rock, and he said unto them, Hear now, ye rebels; must we fetch you water out of this rock?

KJV

Ezek 20:38

38 And I will purge out from among you the rebels, and them that transgress against me: I will bring them forth out of the country where they sojourn, and they shall not enter into the land of Israel: and ye shall know that I am the Lord.

KJV

Isa 59:14

14 And judgment is turned away backward, and justice standeth afar off: for truth is fallen in the street, and equity cannot enter.

KJV

LECTURE NOTES

Message # 831
A HISTORY OF ADAM
(Daniel, Chapter 8)

Part 2

The Prophecies Of Daniel According to Kabbalah, Chapter 8/ Lecture Notes (Part 2)

Appendix – Verse 13

Lecture Notes For Verse 13

¹³ THEN I HEARD ONE SAINT SPEAKING, AND ANOTHER SAINT SAID UNTO THAT CERTAIN SAINT WHICH SPAKE, HOW LONG SHALL BE THE VISION CONCERNING THE DAILY SACRIFICE, AND THE TRANSGRESSION OF DESOLATION, TO GIVE BOTH THE SANCTUARY AND THE HOST TO BE TRODDEN UNDER FOOT?

KJV

Then I heard one holy one/sanctuary (Saint) speaking and said another saint holy one/sanctuary that certain one which spoke, how long the vision the daily [sacrifice] rebellion (transgression) stunned/devastated (desolation) give holy one/Saint (sanctuary) armies (host) abasement/trampled down (trodden underfoot)

Then I heard one holy one speaking and he said to another holy one that certain one which spoke, how long the vision the daily [sacrifice] rebellion stand/devastated give holy one/Saint armies abasement/trampled down

Then I heard one holy one speaking, and the one who spoke said to another holy one, how long do you give it [until] the vision of the daily [sacrifice and] the rebellion [that] stunned and devastated [Righteous Adam and] the armies of the holy ones tread [the 5th day creations] under foot

Then I heard one holy one speaking, and the one who spoke said to another holy one, how long do you give [for] the vision of the daily [sacrifice and] the rebellion [that] stunned and devastated [Righteous Adam to end, and for] the armies of the holy ones to tread [the male Goat] under foot?

The Prophecies Of Daniel According to Kabbalah, Chapter 8/ Lecture Notes (Part 2)

13   Then I heard [Righteous Adam], one holy one speaking, and [Righteous Adam], the one who spoke, said to [Gabriel], another holy one, [explain to Daniel that] the vision [is about] how long [it will take (1) for] the daily [sacrifice and] (2) the rebellion [that] stunned and devastated [Righteous Adam to end, and] (3) to give the armies of the holy ones [the power] to tread [the personality of the Goat] under foot, and (ATB)

Reference Scriptures for Verse 13

Gen 3:17-19

17 And unto Adam he said, Because thou hast hearkened unto the voice of thy wife, and hast eaten of the tree, of which I commanded thee, saying, Thou shalt not eat of it: cursed is the ground for thy sake; in sorrow shalt thou eat of it all the days of thy life;

18 Thorns also and thistles shall it bring forth to thee; and thou shalt eat the herb of the field;

19 In the sweat of thy face shalt thou eat bread, till thou return unto the ground; for out of it wast thou taken: for dust thou art, and unto dust shalt thou return.

KJV

The Prophecies Of Daniel According to Kabbalah, Chapter 8/ Lecture Notes (Part 2)

Appendix – Verse 14

Footnotes

Footnote #38 – Continued

. . . . from where only the inner essence of the blended Sefirot called ***gevurot*** and ***chasidim*** descend into the regenerating Adam within humanity to complete his tzlem image.

The separation of the essence of the blended Names of God from their Sefirotic boundaries in preparation for their descent is called ***the Circumcision of the flesh*** *(Pardes Rimonim, Orchard of Pomegranates,* Part 1, Rabbi Moshe Cordovero*).*

Footnote #39 – Continued

They dwell together as the third degree of power of the God World of Atzilut.

Eventually Adam appeared in the World of Action as a single man, but Adam is a spiritual man who compasses all four worlds. His appearance in the World of Action (Asiyah) is Adam's fourth aspect.

Jehovah formed Adam in the World of Creation (Beriah), breathed the Shekinah, the life of the God World of Emanation (Atzilut) into him, and the Shekinah became Adam's higher mind. But Adam did not have a form, and there are no forms in the World of Emanation (Atzilut) or the World of Creation (Beriah), so, Adam descended into the World of Forms (Yetzirah) where he acquired the spiritual foundation for his material body, and then into the World of Action (Asiyah), where he acquired a material body.

Adam was conscious in all four worlds.

The mind of his flesh body in the World of Action (Asiyah) is called the conscious mind,

The mind of the World of Forms (Yetzirah), also called ***the Astral Plane***, is his subconscious mind,

The mind of the World of Creation (Beriah) is the mind of Malchut of the God World of Emanation (Atzilut), Adam's spiritual intelligence, and

The mind of the Shekinah from the God World of Emanation (Atzilut) is his superconscious, or God mind.

These four aspects of mind manifest as Da'at, Tiferet, Yesod and Malchut, the middle column of the ten Sefirot that represent the nature of God.

> [13] I SAW IN THE NIGHT VISIONS, AND, BEHOLD, ONE LIKE THE SON OF MAN CAME WITH THE CLOUDS OF HEAVEN, AND CAME TO THE ANCIENT OF DAYS, AND THEY BROUGHT HIM NEAR BEFORE HIM.
>
> **KJV**

Luke 5:24

> [24] BUT THAT YE MAY KNOW THAT THE SON OF MAN HATH POWER UPON EARTH TO FORGIVE SINS, (HE SAID UNTO THE SICK OF THE PALSY,) I SAY UNTO THEE, ARISE, AND TAKE UP THY COUCH, AND GO INTO THINE HOUSE.
>
> **KJV**

Lecture Notes For Verse 14

> **14** AND HE SAID UNTO ME, UNTO TWO THOUSAND AND THREE HUNDRED DAYS; THEN SHALL THE SANCTUARY BE CLEANSED.
>
> **KJV**

Said me until (unto) evening (6153) daybreak/morning (1242) (days) 2000 (thousand) three (Binah) hundred made righteous (cleansed) sacred place (sanctuary)

The Prophecies Of Daniel According to Kabbalah, Chapter 8/ Lecture Notes (Part 2)

Said me until evening daybreak/morning 2000 three hundred made righteous sacred place

And he said to me, until the evening and the morning of the second day of creation, [when Binah descends into] the holy ones [and becomes Keter, Chochmah and Binah, their upper] triad, to make [them] righteous,

14 **[Gabriel] said to me, [it will take] until the evening and the morning of the Second Day of Creation, [when the spirit of Binah descends into] the holy ones [to become the Keter, Chochmah and Binah, the upper] triad [of young Adam, the one who] makes [them] righteous, and (ATB)**

Genesis 1:7-8: - AT:

7 And Elohim formed an expanse [that made] a division between the waters which were under the expanse and the waters which were above the expanse, and [that is how Elohim] set [the ignorant, miserable and wicked soul] upright (so),

*8 And Elohim called the expanse Heaven, and the enlightened soul and the first emanations [of Adam Kadmon] were the second day **(ATB)*** (Rendered by Pastor Vitale in Message 829, the Fifth Day Creation – Part 2.)

Reference Scriptures for Verse 14

Matt 9:28

28 And when he was come into the house, the blind men came to him: and Jesus saith unto them, Believe ye that I am able to do this? They said unto him, Yea, Lord.

KJV

Appendix – Verse 15

Lecture Notes For Verse 15

¹⁵ AND IT CAME TO PASS, WHEN I, EVEN I DANIEL, HAD SEEN THE VISION, AND SOUGHT FOR THE MEANING, THEN, BEHOLD, THERE STOOD BEFORE ME AS THE APPEARANCE OF A MAN.

KJV

15   And it came to pass that when Daniel saw I [AM's] vision and sought after the meaning, there it was! A man [who] appeared [to be] a mighty warrior stood opposite him, (ATB)

Appendix – Verse 16

Footnotes

Footnote #41 – Continued

Adam, mankind, is the only mediator between ***humanity, homo sapien man***, and the God world of Atzilut.

Humanity [Mankind] Atzilut

Humanity [Mankind] God who is in Heaven

Humanity [Mankind] Primordial Adam

Earth [Mankind] Heaven

Daniel [Adam] Gabriel

So we see that ***Adam is the man*** that Jehovah formed, and that we, ***humanity, are the earthen vessels*** that Adam dwells in.

The spiritual man, Adam, dwells in the midst of mankind, the visible image of himself.

In verse 16, the spiritual man, Adam, mankind, communicates directly with the angel Gabriel, who is in heaven, instructing him to enlighten Daniel, the earthen ***human*** vessel that he, Adam, the spiritual man, dwells in.

1 Tim 2:5

> [5] FOR THERE IS ONE GOD, AND ONE MEDIATOR BETWEEN GOD AND MEN, THE MAN CHRIST JESUS;
> **KJV**

The spiritual man, Adam, is called ***Christ Jesus*** in the New Testament, where he is clothed in Jesus' personality.

2 Cor 4:6-7

⁶ FOR GOD, WHO COMMANDED THE LIGHT TO SHINE OUT OF DARKNESS, HATH SHINED IN OUR HEARTS, TO GIVE THE LIGHT OF THE KNOWLEDGE OF THE GLORY OF GOD IN THE FACE OF JESUS CHRIST.

⁷ BUT WE HAVE THIS TREASURE IN EARTHEN VESSELS, THAT THE EXCELLENCY OF THE POWER MAY BE OF GOD, AND NOT OF US.

KJV

2 Cor 4:6-7 - AT:

6 Because God who commanded the light [of Primordial Adam] to shine out of the darkness [in Genesis 1:3], has commanded [Primordial Adam], that same [spiritual] light, to shine upon the hearts of humanity, to enlighten us with the knowledge of God's opinion through the personality of Jesus Christ

7 Wherefore, Jehovah gave us [the spiritual man, Adam, the Mediator, to be] a storehouse for [Primordial Adam], the enlightenment [of God's opinion, to dwell in our] earthen vessels, so that the power that goes out from us should be of God, and not [of Satan] **(ATB)**

Gen 2:18

¹⁸ AND THE LORD GOD SAID, IT IS NOT GOOD THAT THE MAN SHOULD BE ALONE; I WILL MAKE HIM AN HELP MEET FOR HIM.

KJV

Genesis 2:18 - AT: *And Jehovah Elohim said, it is not good for Adam, mankind, to be alone, I will make a mate for him to assist* **(ATB)**

The Prophecies Of Daniel According to Kabbalah, Chapter 8/ Lecture Notes (Part 2)

¹⁶ AND I HEARD A MAN'S VOICE BETWEEN THE BANKS OF ULAI, WHICH CALLED, AND SAID, GABRIEL, MAKE THIS MAN TO UNDERSTAND THE VISION.

KJV

And I heard Adam's voice in the midst of (between) the foolish [shepherd] (Ulai) call Gabriel by name, saying, understand this (man not in Hebrew) other self (untranslated word – et) the vision

And I heard Adam's voice in the midst of the foolish [shepherd] call Gabriel by name, saying, understand this other self the vision (ATB)

Reference Scriptures for Verse 16

Ex 35:30

30 And Moses said unto the children of Israel, See, the Lord hath called by name Bezaleel the son of Uri, the son of Hur, of the tribe of Judah;

KJV

John 10:3

3 To him the porter openeth; and the sheep hear his voice: and he calleth his own sheep by name, and leadeth them out.

KJV

The Prophecies Of Daniel According to Kabbalah, Chapter 8/ Lecture Notes (Part 2)

Appendix – Verse 17

Lecture Notes For Verse 17

¹⁷ SO HE CAME NEAR WHERE I STOOD: AND WHEN HE CAME, I WAS AFRAID, AND FELL UPON MY FACE: BUT HE SAID UNTO ME, UNDERSTAND, O SON OF MAN: FOR AT THE TIME OF THE END SHALL BE THE VISION.

KJV

And he came near to where I stood, and when he approached me, I was afraid and my personality (face) fell down

Gen 4:6

⁶ AND THE LORD SAID UNTO CAIN, WHY ART THOU WROTH? AND WHY IS **THY COUNTENANCE FALLEN?**

KJV

17   And he said to me understand, son of Adam, [that] the vision [is about] the end times, (ATB)

The Prophecies Of Daniel According to Kabbalah, Chapter 8/ Lecture Notes (Part 2)

Appendix – Verse 18

Lecture Notes For Verse 18

18 NOW AS HE WAS SPEAKING WITH ME, I WAS IN A DEEP SLEEP ON MY FACE TOWARD THE GROUND: BUT HE TOUCHED ME, AND SET ME UPRIGHT.

KJV

And as he spoke with me I was stunned [and] fell into a trance (deep sleep) and my personality (face forward) earth but he had spiritual sexual intercourse (touched) with me and stood me upright

And as he spoke with me I was stunned [and] fell into a trance and my personality earth but he had spiritual sexual intercourse with me and stood me upright

And I was stunned, [and] as he spoke with me I fell into a trance, and he had spiritual sexual intercourse with my earth[en] personality, [which] stood me upright,

18 I was stunned, [and] as he spoke with me I fell into a trance, and [Gabriel] had spiritual sexual intercourse with my earth[en] personality, [and] stood me upright, (ATB)

The Prophecies Of Daniel According to Kabbalah, Chapter 8/ Lecture Notes (Part 2)

Appendix – Verse 19

Footnotes

Footnote #43 - Continued

. . . . are influenced by **_Elohim, God_**, and are called **_sheep_**. Gabriel is telling Daniel that he has two sides: The **_goat_** personality that he was born with and the **_God_** personality called, **_sheep_**. See, also, Notes 39 and 41.

Lecture Notes For Verse 19

> [19] AND HE SAID, BEHOLD, I WILL MAKE THEE KNOW WHAT SHALL BE IN THE LAST END OF THE INDIGNATION: FOR AT THE TIME APPOINTED THE END SHALL BE.
>
> **KJV**

And he said, look! I will make you to know Elohim, your other self (other=what) (834) self (853)) shall be at the end of the fury (indignation) appointed time of the end

And he said, look! I will make you to know Elohim, your other self shall come to pass (be) at the end of the fury/rage appointed time of the end

And he said, look! I will tell you [what] shall come to pass at the appointed time of the end, [when] Elohim, your other self, [shall put] an end [to Cain's] rage,

19   [Gabriel] said, look! I will tell you [what] shall come to pass at the appointed time of the end, [when] Elohim, your other self, [shall put] an end [to Cain's] rage [which is revealed through the kings of the earth, because], (ATB)

The Prophecies Of Daniel According to Kabbalah, Chapter 8/ Lecture Notes (Part 2)

Reference Scriptures for Verse 19

Gen 4:6

6 And the Lord said unto Cain, Why art thou wroth? and why is thy countenance fallen? KJV

Appendix – Verse 20

Footnotes

Footnote #47 – Continued

. . . . between good and evil, so they were destroyed, but they rose again in a balanced form in the God World of Emanation (Atzilut).

Their unbalanced mirror image appeared in the World of Action (Asiyah) as the Kings of Edom (Gen3631-39:, all of which died, except one, whose negative spiritual strength will be balanced by King Messiah and the forces of spiritual Israel.

Lecture Notes For Verse 20

> [20] THE RAM WHICH THOU SAWEST HAVING TWO HORNS ARE THE KINGS OF MEDIA AND PERSIA.
>
> **KJV**

The mighty man (ram) that you saw [who] had two sources of power, are the kings of

OT:4078 - Media

OT:4074 מָדַי **Maday** (maw-dah'-ee); of foreign derivation; Madai, a country of central Asia:

KJV - Madai, Medes, Media.

The Prophecies Of Daniel According to Kabbalah, Chapter 8/ Lecture
Notes (Part 2)

SAME LETTERS – DIFERENT VOWELS

OT:4075 מָדַי **Maday** (maw-dah'-ee); patrial from OT:4074; a Madian or native of Madai:

KJV - Mede.

OT:4076 מָדַי **Maday** (Aramaic) (maw-dah'-ee); corresponding to OT:4074:

KJV - Mede (-s).

OT:4077 מָדַי **Maday** (Aramaic) (maw-dah'-ee); corresponding to OT:4075:

KJV - Median.

OT:4078 מַדַּי **madday** (mad-dah'-ee); from OT:4100 and OT:1767; what (is) enough, i.e. **sufficiently**:

(Biblesoft's New Exhaustive Strong's Numbers and Concordance with Expanded Greek-Hebrew Dictionary. Copyright © 1994, 2003, 2006 Biblesoft, Inc. and International Bible Translators, Inc.)

OT:6535 - Persia

OT:6536 פָּרַס **parac** (paw-ras'); a primitive root; **to break in pieces**, i.e. (usually without violence) to split, distribute:

KJV - deal, divide, have hoofs, part, tear.

OT:6537 פְּרַס **perac** (Aramaic) (per-as'); corresponding to OT:6536; **to split up**:

KJV - divide, [U-] pharsin.

OT:6538 פֶּרֶס **perec** (peh'-res); from OT:6536; a claw; also **a kind of eagle**:

KJV - claw, ossifrage.

OT:6539 פָּרַס **Parac** (paw-ras'); of foreign origin; Paras (i.e. Persia), an Eastern country, including its inhabitants:

KJV - Persia, Persians.

OT:6540 פָּרַס **Parac** (Aramaic) (paw-ras'); corresponding to OT:6539:

KJV - Persia, Persians.

(Biblesoft's New Exhaustive Strong's Numbers and Concordance with Expanded Greek-Hebrew Dictionary. Copyright © 1994, 2003, 2006 Biblesoft, Inc. and International Bible Translators, Inc.)

The mighty man (ram) that you saw [who] had two sources of power, are the kings of sufficient break in pieces

The mighty man that you saw [who] had two sources of power, are the kings of sufficient break in pieces

The Prophecies Of Daniel According to Kabbalah, Chapter 8/ Lecture Notes (Part 2)

[The Mother and the Son of the God World of Atzilut], the two sources of power of [Righteous Adam], the mighty man that you saw, are sufficient to break the kings [who fell down from the World of Points] in pieces,

[The Mother and the Son of the God World of Atzilut], the two sources of power of [Righteous Adam], the mighty man that you saw, are sufficient to break the kings [of this world] in pieces, and

20 [The Mother and the Son of the God World of Atzilut], the two sources of power of [Righteous Adam], the mighty man that you saw, are sufficient to break [the power of] the kings [of the earth] in pieces, and (ATB)

Job 3:14

[14] WITH **KINGS** AND COUNSELLORS **OF THE EARTH**, WHICH BUILT DESOLATE PLACES FOR THEMSELVES;

KJV

Ps 2:2-3

[2] THE **KINGS OF THE EARTH** SET THEMSELVES, AND THE RULERS TAKE COUNSEL TOGETHER, AGAINST THE LORD, AND AGAINST HIS ANOINTED, SAYING,

[3] LET US BREAK THEIR BANDS ASUNDER, AND CAST AWAY THEIR CORDS FROM US.

KJV

Isa 24:21

²¹ And it shall come to pass in that day, that the Lord shall punish the host of the high ones that are on high, and the **KINGS OF THE EARTH** upon the earth.

KJV

Acts 4:26

²⁶ The **KINGS OF THE EARTH** stood up, and the rulers were gathered together against the Lord, and against his Christ.

KJV

Rev 16:14

¹⁴ For they are the spirits of devils, working miracles, which go forth unto the **KINGS OF THE EARTH** and of the whole world, to gather them to the battle of that great day of God Almighty.

KJV

Rev 17:2

² With whom the **KINGS OF THE EARTH** have committed fornication, and the inhabitants of the earth have been made drunk with the wine of her fornication.

KJV

Rev 18:3

³ For all nations have drunk of the wine of the wrath of her fornication, and the **KINGS OF THE EARTH** have committed fornication with her, and the merchants of

The Prophecies Of Daniel According to Kabbalah, Chapter 8/ Lecture Notes (Part 2)

THE EARTH ARE WAXED RICH THROUGH THE ABUNDANCE OF HER DELICACIES.

KJV

Rev 19:19

[19] AND I SAW THE BEAST, AND THE **KINGS OF THE EARTH**, AND THEIR ARMIES, GATHERED TOGETHER TO MAKE WAR AGAINST HIM THAT SAT ON THE HORSE, AND AGAINST HIS ARMY.

KJV

The Prophecies Of Daniel According to Kabbalah, Chapter 8/ Lecture Notes (Part 2)

Appendix – Verse 21

Footnotes

Footnote #46 – Continued

. . . . David was the third king to be an incarnation of Righteous Adam in the earth and Messiah will be the fourth and final king.

Lecture Notes For Verse 21

> [21] AND THE ROUGH GOAT IS THE KING OF GRECIA: AND THE GREAT HORN THAT IS BETWEEN HIS EYES IS THE FIRST KING.
>
> **KJV**

Goat faun (rough)

faun

[fawn]

Spell Syllables

- Examples
- Word Origin

noun, Classical Mythology

1.
one of a class of rural deities represented as men with the ears, horns, tail, and later also the hind legs of a goat.

The Prophecies Of Daniel According to Kabbalah, Chapter 8/ Lecture Notes (Part 2)

King of Grecia

OT:3119 - Grecia

OT:3120 יָוָן **Yavan** (yaw-vawn'); probably from the same as OT:3196; effervescing (i.e. hot and active); Javan, the name of a son of Joktan, and of the race (Ionians, i.e. Greeks) descended from him, with their territory; also of a place in Arabia:

KJV - Javan.

OT:3121 יָוֵן **yaven** (yaw-ven'); from the same as OT:3196; properly, **dregs** (as effervescing); hence, **mud**:

KJV - mire, miry.

(Biblesoft's New Exhaustive Strong's Numbers and Concordance with Expanded Greek-Hebrew Dictionary. Copyright © 1994, 2003, 2006 Biblesoft, Inc. and International Bible Translators, Inc.)

Goat faun (rough) King mud

> [21] THE KING [THAT IS] FORMED FROM THE MUD LOOKS LIKE A MAN, BUT IS AN HYBRID DEITY THAT HAS HORNS, A TAIL AND THE HIND LEGS OF A GOAT, AND THE GREAT POWER (HORN) BETWEEN HIS TWO EYES IS [NIMROD], THE FIRST KING,

21 **The king [that is] formed from the mud, [who] looks like a man, but is [really] an hybrid deity that has horns, a tail and the hind legs of a goat, and the great power between his two eyes is [Nimrod], the first king, and (ATB)**

The Prophecies Of Daniel According to Kabbalah, Chapter 8/ Lecture Notes (Part 2)

Appendix – Verse 22

Footnotes

Footnote 45 – Continued

.... of the four worlds above: Emanation (Atzilut), Creation (Beriah), Forms (Yetzirah) and Action (Asiyah)

Lecture Notes For Verse 22

> [22] NOW THAT BEING BROKEN, WHEREAS FOUR STOOD UP FOR IT, FOUR KINGDOMS SHALL STAND UP OUT OF THE NATION, BUT NOT IN HIS POWER.
>
> **KJV**

In the window of the fish (prefices vav, nun, heh) burst (now that being broken) and the serpent (prefices vav tet) stood up four [worlds] below four kingdoms nations stand up not large lizard (power)

In the [lower] window of [creation where] the fish [is], a large lizard burst [apart] the two powers of [Righteous Adam] and the Serpent stood up four nations below [to replace] the four [spiritual] kingdoms [that exist, but] are not standing up [and visible in this world yet]

22 **A large Lizard burst [apart the Mother and the Son], the two powers [which were revealed through Righteous Adam] in the [lower] window of [creation where Leviathan], the fish [is], and the Serpent stood up four nations [in the world] below [to replace] the four [spiritual] kingdoms [that exist, but] are not standing up [and visible in this world yet, but] (ATB)**

The Prophecies Of Daniel According to Kabbalah, Chapter 8/ Lecture Notes (Part 2)

Reference Scriptures for Verse 22

Rev 17:12
12 And the ten horns which thou sawest are ten kings, which have received no kingdom as yet; but receive power as kings one hour with the beast.

KJV

The Prophecies Of Daniel According to Kabbalah, Chapter 8/ Lecture Notes (Part 2)

Appendix – Verse 23

Footnotes

Footnote #48 – Continued

In the last days of this age, King Messiah, the personification of Primordial Adam, who is the Keter, shall appear to transfer the spiritual DNA of Primordial Adam to Righteous Adam, who is regenerating in the members of the Israel of God.

Footnote #49 – Continued

. . . . to have an adult conversation with Righteous Adam, the only Mediator between God and man.

God speaks to Righteous Adam and Righteous Adam speaks to the spiritual intelligence within us. Where there is no spiritual intelligence, substantive communication with God is not possible.

This spiritual intelligence is the female seed that was lowered into the earth before time began. It is the spiritual bone structure upon which Jehovah formed Adam's dust. It is called **malchus**, because it is the reproductive essence of the God World of Emanation (Atzilut), the spiritual DNA of that world which was delivered to the World of Creation (Beriah) through the Malchut of the higher world, by the Circumcision of the Flesh. (See, also, Note 38)

Lecture Notes For Verse 23

²³ AND IN THE LATTER TIME OF THEIR KINGDOM, WHEN THE TRANSGRESSORS ARE COME TO THE FULL, A KING OF FIERCE COUNTENANCE, AND UNDERSTANDING DARK SENTENCES, SHALL STAND UP.

KJV

The Prophecies Of Daniel According to Kabbalah, Chapter 8/ Lecture Notes (Part 2)

In the end time (and in the latter time of) their kingdom complete (when are come to the full) to trespass (transgressors) shall stand up a king with procreative power

OT:5794 - power

5794. עַז **'az:**

I. An adjective meaning strong, powerful; insolent. When referring to a person's attitude of anger or wrath, it means insolent, excessive, fierce (Gen 49:7); used of physical strength or power, it means strong, forceful (Ex 14:21; Judges 14:14). The phrase ±*az p'nîm*, strong of faces means determined, defiant (Deut 28:50; Dan 8:23); in context ±*az ne,eš* indicates that persons are greedy, covetous, insatiable (Isa 56:11). Describing bold or arrogant speech, it means arrogantly, insolently (Prov 18:23). Ants are not considered strong but are wise (Prov 30:25). Used as a noun, it means a strong person (Amos 5:9).

II. A masculine noun meaning power, strength. It is used as an abstract noun to refer to **procreative power and the power of offspring** (Gen 49:3).

I.

Gen. 49:7; **Ex.** 14:21; **Num.** 13:28; 21:24; **Deut.** 28:50; **Judg.** 14:14,18; **2 Sam.** 22:18; **Neh.** 9:11; **Ps.** 18:17(18); 59:3(4); **Prov.** 18:23; 21:14; 30:25; **Song** 8:6; **Isa.** 19:4; 25:3; 43:16; 56:11; **Ezek.** 7:24; **Dan.** 8:23; **Amos** 5:9.

II.

Gen. 49:3.

(from The Complete Word Study Dictionary: Old Testament Copyright © 2003 by AMG Publishers. All rights reserved.)

In the end time (and in the latter time of) their kingdom complete (when are come to the full) to trespass/rebel (transgressors) shall stand up a king with procreative power personality (countenance) understanding/intelligence enigma/riddle/mysteries (dark sentences)

The Prophecies Of Daniel According to Kabbalah, Chapter 8/ Lecture
Notes (Part 2)

In the end time their kingdom complete rebels shall stand up a king with procreative power personality understanding/intelligence riddles

23   In the end time, a King with [spiritual] procreative power and the [spiritual] intelligence to understand the mysteries of the kingdom [of God], shall stand up and complete the personalities of the rebels, (ATB)

Appendix – Verse 24

Lecture Notes For Verse 24

²⁴ AND HIS POWER SHALL BE MIGHTY, BUT NOT BY HIS OWN POWER: AND HE SHALL DESTROY WONDERFULLY, AND SHALL PROSPER, AND PRACTISE, AND SHALL DESTROY THE MIGHTY AND THE HOLY PEOPLE.

KJV

And shall be mighty the large lizard (power) not power to separate/distinguish by implication (wonderfully) decay (destroy) push forward (prosper) to do/make (practice) decay/ruin (destroy) powerful/numerous (mighty)

And shall be mighty the large lizard not power to separate/distinguish by implication decay push forward to do/make decay/ruin powerful/numerous

24 And the large lizard shall be mighty, and [Righteous Adam shall not have the power to separate [himself from the male goat, but the Shekinah] shall push forward [into the earth], and destroy [the Lizard that empowers the male Goat, and Righteous Adam] shall make [the male Goat and] a large number of [the female goats, into] a ruin[ous heap], (ATB)

The Prophecies Of Daniel According to Kabbalah, Chapter 8/ Lecture Notes (Part 2)

Appendix – Verse 25

Footnotes

Footnote #55 – Continued

. . . . Everything created on the previous Days were to be a part of the final product. The reptilian species, however, refused to submit to Elohim's design and have been waging a war against Jehovah Elohim and Adam, the Sixth Day Creation, ever since

Lecture Notes For Verse 25

> ^{25} AND THROUGH HIS POLICY ALSO HE SHALL CAUSE CRAFT TO PROSPER IN HIS HAND; AND HE SHALL MAGNIFY HIMSELF IN HIS HEART, AND BY PEACE SHALL DESTROY MANY: HE SHALL ALSO STAND UP AGAINST THE PRINCE OF PRINCES; BUT HE SHALL BE BROKEN WITHOUT HAND.
>
> **KJV**

Above (though also) intelligence (policy) push forward what (and he shall cause to prosper) deceit/fraud (craft) hand heart twist (magnify) peace destroy/ruin many above (against) the Prince of princes stand up the end/no further

Above intelligence push for deceit/fraud mind (hand) heart twist peace destroy/ruin many above the Prince of princes stand up the end/no further

[And the Shekinah], the intelligence from above, shall push forward into the heart [center of] the counterfeit [Adam], and the mind of peace from above shall twist together with [fallen Adam's] ruined [mind, and] the Prince of princes shall stand up in the many [members of mankind, and] the rebellion shall end (proceed no further)

25   And the Shekinah, Jehovah's] intelligence from above, shall push forward into the heart [center of] the counterfeit [Adam], and the mind from above [that is at] peace [with Jehovah], shall twist together with [fallen Adam's] ruined [mind, and] the Prince of princes shall stand up in the many [members of mankind, and] end the rebellion, and (ATB)

Reference Scriptures for Verse 25

Eph 2:15

15 Having abolished in his flesh the enmity, even the law of commandments contained in ordinances; for to make in himself of twain one new man, so making peace;

KJV

Appendix – Verse 26

Lecture Notes For Verse 26

²⁶ AND THE VISION OF THE EVENING AND THE MORNING WHICH WAS TOLD IS TRUE: WHEREFORE SHUT THOU UP THE VISION; FOR IT SHALL BE FOR MANY DAYS.

KJV

26   And the vision of the evening and the morning [of the Second Day of Creation] which was told to you is true, [but] the vision will not come to pass for many days, so [the understanding of it] will be locked up [until the time appointed for it to come to pass], (ATB)

The Prophecies Of Daniel According to Kabbalah, Chapter 8/ Lecture Notes (Part 2)

Appendix – Verse 27

Footnotes

Footnote #57 – Continued

. . . . to be joined permanently with the Spirit of Messiah. But the fallen nature must be purged before the final union takes place, because it is a spiritual perversion for a man to have two natures. Such a condition can only be temporary. One of the two natures must fully dominate the vessel and the other must die. The New Inner Man, which is being built in righteousness, sustains the physical body as the Old Inner Man dies.

Daniel did not understand the vision, means that the wisdom of the Word of God did not form the Son of Adam within Daniel. So, when the creative process weakened Daniel's Old Inner Man, there was no New Inner Man to sustain Daniel's strength, and Daniel fell ill.

Lecture Notes For Verse 27

> [27] AND I DANIEL FAINTED, AND WAS SICK CERTAIN DAYS; AFTERWARD I ROSE UP, AND DID THE KING'S BUSINESS; AND I WAS ASTONISHED AT THE VISION, BUT NONE UNDERSTOOD IT.
>
> **KJV**

And I Daniel to be (fainted) weak days the head (prefix alef*) stood up (afterward I rose up) and did mate (untranslated et) the king's creative process (business) and I was destroyed from above vision not understood

* The letter alef ("a") can be translated ***thousand***, the number associated with **Chochmah**, *wisdom of the father*:

The Prophecies Of Daniel According to Kabbalah, Chapter 8/ Lecture Notes (Part 2)

OT:505 - alef

505. אֶלֶף 'ele,: A masculine noun meaning **a thousand** or clan. The word was commonly used for people, weights (including money), measures, and livestock (Judg 8:26; 2 though the word is usually literal, sometimes it is used poetically to suggest a large number (Gen 24:60; Job 9:3). In a few cases, it carries the sense of an extended family or clan (Judg 6:15).

(from The Complete Word Study Dictionary: Old Testament Copyright © 2003 by AMG Publishers. All rights reserved.)

And I Daniel to be weak days wisdom stood up mate the king's business and I was destroyed from above vision not understood

And Daniel was physically weak [for many] days [after Righteous Adam, the Son of] I [AM], stood up, [because Righteous Adam, Daniel's] mate from above, is the creative process that destroys the king[dom of darkness, [but Daniel] did not understand the vision

COMMENT: The Doctrine of Christ destroys our old man and builds the son of God in us, but only if we understand it. To hear the doctrine without understanding produces sickness in the physical body without building Righteous Adam who is our new life and health by him.

The people who died while in this ministry did not understand what was being taught. What is being taught is confession of sin and repentance. After that, the promise of longevity and eternal life. Many hear only the promise of eternal life, but the message of confession and repentance escape them because of the sins of idolatry and pride.

27   And Daniel was physically weak [for many] days [after Righteous Adam, Daniel's] mate from above, stood up [in him, because] the DNA of I [AM] destroys the king[dom of darkness, and Daniel] did not understand the vision (ATB)

TABLE OF REFERENCES

1

1 Kings 8:20 34
1 Tim 2:5 71

2

2 Cor 4:6-7 72

A

Acts 17:28 39
Acts 4:26 82

D

Dan 10:13 56
Dan 10:21 56
Dan 12:1 .... 56, 60
Dan 7:13 .... 33, 55
Dan 7:2 31
Deut 6:8 46

E

Eph 2:15 93
Ex 35:30 73
Ezek 1:10 51
Ezek 10:14 52
Ezek 2:1 32
Ezek 20:38 62
Ezek 38:3 57

G

Gen 1:27 48
Gen 2:10 38
Gen 2:18 .... 45, 72
Gen 3:14-15 43
Gen 3:16 43
Gen 3:17-19 .... 42, 66
Gen 3:6 42
Gen 4:5 48

Gen 4:6 .... 74, 77
Gen 6:1-2 .... 40, 41, 53
Gen 9:2 41

I

Isa 24:21 82
Isa 59:14 62

J

Job 3:14 81
John 10:3 73
John 10:7 38
John 10:9 38

L

Luke 5:24 .... 33, 68

M

Mal 4:3 .... 49, 50, 58
Matt 19:28 54
Matt 9:28 69

N

Num 20:10 62
Num 28:2-6 59

P

Ps 2:2-3 81

R

Rev 12:7 57
Rev 16:14 82
Rev 17:12 87
Rev 17:2 82
Rev 18:3 82
Rev 19:19 83
Rom 1:23 47

S

Song 2:2.....................................33
Song 2:9.....................................55

Z

Zech 11:15 35

ABOUT THE AUTHOR

Sheila R. Vitale is the Spiritual Leader, Founding Teacher, and Pastor of Living Epistles Ministries (*LEM*) and Christ-Centered Kabbalah (*CCK*). A brief history of Pastor Vitale and the unique two-pronged ministry that the Lord Jesus Christ gave her charge over (*LEM/CCK*) is encapsulated below

She moves in the offices of Teacher of Apostolic Doctrine, Prophet, Evangelist and Pastor, has an international following, and has been expounding on the Scripture through a unique spiritual lens for nearly three decades. She has written more than 50 books based on the Old and New Testaments including *The Kabbalah of The 1st Epistle of John* and *the Crime of the Calf* (OT) and *The Three Israels* and *Jesus and The Learned Jew* (NT*)*. She has also rendered original spiritual interpretations of Biblical texts such as *The Prophesies of Daniel According to Kabbalah, Chapter 11,* and *The Noah Chronicles*. Her unique, Multi-Part Message style is seen in *CCK* Serial Messages such as Reincarnation vs Transmigration (22 Parts) and Exodus, Chapter 32 (26 Parts). Each Part of a Multi-Part Message Series can also be enjoyed as a complete and independent study. In addition, she has defined, explained, illustrated and demonstrated hundreds of spiritual principles throughout more than 1,000 CCK lectures.

Her signature work, however, is the three volumes of *The Alternate Translation Bible (ATB)*: *The Alternate Translation Of The Old Testament, The Alternate Translation of the New Testament* and *The Alternate Translation of The Book of Revelation. The Alternate Translation Bible* is a work in progress (*The ATB Project*). Accordingly, additional spiritual interpretations of both whole and partial Chapters are added from time to time, as they are rendered. The most up-to-date versions of *The ATB Project* may be found online at the *LEM and CCK* websites: *LivingEpistles.org and Christ-CenteredKabbalah.org*, respectively. *The ATB* is a *spiritual interpretation* of the Scripture and is not intended to replace traditional translations.

She also analyzed the Greek text of *The Book of Revelation* and preached extensively on it in the early years of *The ATB Project*. During that time she produced 197 distinct *Message Parts*, under 29 specific *Message Titles*, all of which deal with *The Book of Revelation*.

Pastor Vitale is an illustrator of spiritual principles, a researcher, a translator and a reviewer of the Modern Social Trends of Family and Culture, as they are revealed through TV programs (*The Sopranos*), movies (*The Matrix* and *The Edge of Tomorrow*), and plays (*Wicked*). She also writes for the CCK *Blog*.

She travels domestically, as well as internationally, preaching and teaching Judeo-Christian Spiritual Philosophy, and has donated Audio Message Libraries of her Lectures to ministries in Asia, Africa, Europe and North America.

Pastor Vitale serves *CCK* in a range of spiritual, educational, and administrative functions from *The Selden Centre, LEM/CCK* headquarters in Selden, New York. She is also a philanthropic individual who supports the *Lighthouse Mission* (Patchogue, NY) and *HGM – Mission of Hope – Haiti, and other* charitable organizations. She also supports community services such as the *Terryville Fire Department*.

In her spare time, Pastor Vitale enjoys watching movies, attending plays and partaking of cuisines from different cultures. An avid traveler, she has visited several countries in Europe and Africa as well as many cities in the United States.

BEGINNINGS, INSPIRATION AND CALLING

Pastor Vitale began her spiritual journey as a child when her Jewish mother enrolled her in the Hebrew school of an Orthodox synagogue. She experienced the Spirit of God for the first time there in such a profound way that she wept. But after that, when she was only eleven years old, she became very ill and was taken to Mount Sinai Hospital in New York City. She almost died there and has battled with life-threatening health issues ever since. Nevertheless, a deep longing for God continued to pursue her until several years later when she desperately wanted to attend Yeshiva (Jewish high school), but could not. Her secular parents approved of her choice but were not able to afford the tuition.

Much later, after years of searching, she once again experienced the Spirit that had brought her to tears in the synagogue of her youth, but this time it was at *Gospel Revivals Ministries*, a Pentecostal church where Deliverance Ministry was emphasized. She desired to understand the Bible since she was a child, but Scripture was difficult for her and she struggled with the text. Nevertheless, she read one Chapter of the Bible every day until, one day, *her spiritual eyes opened* and she saw an angel holding a little book.

After that, she attended as many as five teaching services each week for about seven years, the latter part of which she edited *Pastor Holzhauser's* books. But several more years had to pass before *the eyes of her understanding opened even further* and she began to receive *Revelation Knowledge of the Scripture*. She understood at that time that the angel she had seen was the angel of Revelation 10:8.

After about seven years of learning *Deliverance Ministry* and *The Doctrine of Sonship* (*Bill Britton*) from *Pastor*

Holzhauser, she studied the Bible independently under the influence and direction of the Holy Spirit.

In **1988** she began teaching Apostolic Doctrine.

In **1990** she spent three months in Stony Brook Hospital where she recovered from an incurable disease, defeating premature death, once again, and went on to resume teaching and managing *LEM.*

In **1992** she journeyed to Africa for the first time where she was called to the office of Evangelist.

In the **mid-1990s,** she began to Pastor in addition to being a Teacher of Apostolic Doctrine, a Prophet and an Evangelist, thus, satisfying all five offices of *The Ministry of the Lord Jesus Christ to His Church.*

LIVING EPISTLES MINISTRIES

Pastor Vitale was happy fellowshipping at *Gospel Revivals Ministries* but, eventually, she desired a deeper and more spiritual understanding of the Word of God. One day, after crying out to Jesus about her need, she was amazed to hear Him ask her if she would teach. Her initial response was that she did not see how it would be possible since she was already working a full-time job, despite her poor health. But after the Lord asked her for a second and then a third time, she reluctantly agreed, believing that He would empower her to do the job. Shortly thereafter, in the latter part of 1987, she began to teach her own brand of Judeo-Christian Spiritual Philosophy.

The Lord Jesus Christ named the work *Living Epistles Ministries* in 1988.

The first *LEM* meetings were casual and spontaneous gatherings of friends and fellow deliverance workers in Pastor Vitale's home. After that, they were held in the business office of one of the brethren. Pastor Vitale delivered her first formal message entitled *The Truth About Witchcraft in January of 1988*, followed by *The Seduction of Eve* in April of the same year. After that, she prepared and taught weekly messages including *Signs of Apostleship* and *Lazarus & The Rich Man*. The meetings eventually increased to two and then three each week.

Sometime after that, she learned that the Lord Jesus Christ was revealing spiritual principles from the Hebrew text of the Old Testament through her teachings, and those spiritual principles helped her to begin to unlock the mysteries of the New Testament, as well. Today she understands that the Scripture is a spiritual document that must be spiritually discerned if it is to be understood correctly, and calls that spiritual understanding ***The Doctrine of Christ***.

CHRIST-CENTERED KABBALAH

Another Beginning

After about ten years of teaching *the Doctrine of Christ*, in or about the year 2000, while she was evangelizing in Greenville, South Carolina, the Lord Jesus Christ introduced Pastor Vitale to *Lurian Kabbalah*. At that time, the Spirit of God directed her to read and study the teachings of *Rabbi Luria*, as written by his student, *Chayyim Vital*, in *The Tree of Life: The Palace of Adam Kadmon*. She did not understand the text at first, but continued on, nevertheless, until *the eyes of her understanding opened*.

Shortly thereafter, she began to teach *Lurian Kabbalah* and eventually applied the spiritual principles of that system to her studies in the Old Testament under the *Living Epistles Ministries* brand. Sometime in or about the year 2001, however, the Lord Jesus Christ named her, then current teachings, Christ-centered Kabbalah (*CCK*), thereby dividing *Living Epistles Ministries* into two branches, each with its own website and digital representations. Each ministry has its own label, but both also share the *LEM/CCK* moniker.

About CCK

Christ-Centered Kabbalah is a new, vigorous approach to spiritual maturity, ascension and rectification (justification) based on Pastor Vitale's original research in *the Hebrew text of the Torah, the Greek text of the New Testament* and *the Zohar*, one of the foundational books of *Philosophical Kabbalah.*

CCK, an integration of the *Doctrine of Christ* and *Lurian Kabbalah*, two Bible-based philosophical systems, offers a fresh perspective concerning Israel's resurrection and Adam's restoration to a higher estate than the one he fell from.

She has studied the authentic Jewish Kabbalah of several Rabbinic scholars, including *Moses Nachmanides (Ramban), Moses Cordovero (Ramak)* and *Isaac Luria (The Ari) and* has read many of the English translations of their writings, including *Ramban's The Gate of Reward, Ramak's Pardes Rimonim (Orchard of Pomegranates),* and *the* teachings *of the Ari*, as written by his student, *Chayyim Vital: The Gate of Reincarnations* and *The Tree of Life: The Palace of Adam Kadmon.* Pastor Vitale attributes her ability to understand and teach authentic *Jewish Kabbalah* and *Christ-Centered Kabbalah,* which she believes is beyond the grasp of the human mind, to *The Lord Jesus Christ.*

Pastor Vitale cautions her students about the dangers of *Occult Qabalah* and warns everyone with ears to hear that all Kabbalah is not kosher (authentic). Pastor Vitale teaches *authentic Jewish Kabbalah, which glorifies God* and shuns the *occult Qabalah of personal power,* which, all too frequently, is used to control unsuspecting persons, acquire wealth by spiritual power, or punish one's enemies.

Media

CCK publishes a wide range of material, including books, e-books, spiritual interpretations of the Scripture and transcripts of Pastor Vitale's *Christ-Centered Kaballah* Lectures. Many of her transcripts and the entire *Alternate Translation Bible* may be viewed without charge on the *CCK Website* (*Christ-CenteredKaballah.org*).

She also has an *Author's Website* where all of her books, as well as several photographs of herself and a short biography are displayed (Amazon.com/author/SheilaVitale). Paperback and digital versions of *CCK* books may be purchased through *Amazon, Google Books* and *Barnes & Noble. CCK* also provides free videos of her live streams through YouTube: *@Christ-CenteredKabbalah),* and other Internet Plat-forms.

PASTOR VITALE TODAY

Today Pastor Vitale continues to dedicate her life to teaching the spiritual principles of the Bible and focuses daily on studying, writing and preaching powerful messages from *The Selden Centre,* LEM/CCK's headquarters at Selden, New York.

The Prophecies of Daniel According to Kabbalah, CHAPTER 8, Alternate Translation, is an annotated, esoteric exposition of Daniel's vision of the Ram and the He-Goat.

Mind, Hell & Death, is a deep study which includes Alternate Translations of Dan 8:4-9, 13-14, 19-27, and Rom 5:5-7.

Christ-Centered Kabbalah
Sheila R Vitale,
Pastor, Teacher & Founder
~ The Compleat Kabbalah ~
PO Box 562, Port Jefferson Station, New York 11776, USA
Christ-CenteredKabbalah.org or Books@Christ-CenteredKabbalah.org

www.ingramcontent.com/pod-product-compliance
Lightning Source LLC
Chambersburg PA
CBHW070502100426
42743CB00010B/1723